New Directions for
Adult and Continuing
Education

Susan Imel
Jovita M. Ross-Gordon
COEDITORS-IN-CHIEF

Teaching for Change

Fostering Transformative
Learning in the Classroom

Edward W. Taylor

EDITOR

Number 109 • Spring 2006
Jossey-Bass
San Francisco

TEACHING FOR CHANGE:
FOSTERING TRANSFORMATIVE LEARNING IN THE CLASSROOM
Edward W. Taylor (ed.)
New Directions for Adult and Continuing Education, no. 109
Susan Imel, Jovita M. Ross-Gordon, Coeditors-in-Chief

Microfilm copies of issues and articles are available in 16mm and 35mm, as well as microfiche in 105mm, through University Microfilms Inc., 300 North Zeeb Road, Ann Arbor, Michigan 48106-1346.

NEW DIRECTIONS FOR ADULT AND CONTINUING EDUCATION (ISSN 1052-2891, electronic ISSN 1536-0717) is part of The Jossey-Bass Higher and Adult Education Series and is published quarterly by Wiley Subscription Services, Inc., A Wiley Company, at Jossey-Bass, 989 Market Street, San Francisco, California 94103-1741. Periodicals Postage Paid at San Francisco, California, and at additional mailing offices. POSTMASTER: Send address changes to New Directions for Adult and Continuing Education, Jossey-Bass, 989 Market Street, San Francisco, California 94103-1741.

SUBSCRIPTIONS cost $80.00 for individuals and $180.00 for institutions, agencies, and libraries.

EDITORIAL CORRESPONDENCE should be sent to the Coeditors-in-Chief, Susan Imel, ERIC/ACVE, 1900 Kenny Road, Columbus, Ohio 43210-1090, e-mail: imel.1@osu.edu; or Jovita M. Ross-Gordon, Southwest Texas State University, EAPS Dept., 601 University Drive, San Marcos, TX 78666.

Cover photograph by Jack Hollingsworth@Photodisc

www.josseybass.com

Contents

EDITOR'S NOTES

Fostering transformative learning is about teaching for change. It is learning "predicated on the idea that students are seriously challenged to assess their value system and worldview and are subsequently changed by the experience" (Quinnan, 1997, p. 42). Teaching for change is not an approach to be taken lightly, arbitrarily, or without much thought. Many would argue that it requires intentional action, a willingness to take personal risk, a genuine concern for the learner's betterment, and the wherewithal to draw on a variety of methods and techniques that help create a classroom environment that encourages and supports personal growth. Teaching for change is not easy work, and rewards at times are few, particularly when students are resistant to change.

What makes the work of transformative learning even more difficult is the lack of clear signposts or guidelines that teachers can follow when they try to teach for change. At times it is like groping around in the dark, relying on your intuition and hoping that what you are doing will be appreciated and make a difference in the lives of students. Also, if you are persistent, you eventually overstep your bounds or create conditions that your students are not ready for. Even when guidelines are provided, they are often listed as broad premises that can be interpreted from a variety of perspectives. And every class is different, shaped by the students, by the institutional context, and by what is shaping society at that time. Teaching for change is like starting fresh every time you begin a new course.

One source of guidance can be found through reviewing the research on fostering transformative learning. There is much support for promoting rational discourse and critical reflection, ideal goals for transformative learning (Mezirow and Associates, 2000). In addition, there are other factors of importance, such as fostering group ownership and individual agency, providing intense shared experiential activities, capitalizing on the interrelationship of critical reflection and affective learning, promoting value-laden course content, developing awareness of personal and social contextual influences, and addressing the need for significant amounts of time, all of which reveal a complex and challenging form of teaching (Taylor, 2000).

A more recent critique of research on transformative learning reveals that most studies confirm previous findings along with introducing new approaches for fostering transformative learning (Taylor, 2003). For example, Jarvis (1999) has been successful through the deconstruction of romantic fiction with women in an Access Higher Education Program. She found novels to be a powerful tool in helping women question traditional conceptions of romantic relationships and redefine power located in relationships.

NEW DIRECTIONS FOR ADULT AND CONTINUING EDUCATION, no. 109, Spring 2006 © 2006 Wiley Periodicals, Inc.
Published online in Wiley InterScience (www.interscience.wiley.com) • DOI: 10.1002/ace.202

She concluded, "literary texts offer scope for examining and validating experience, but also for challenging the way experience is constructed and understood" (p. 49). In addition, several studies began to identify factors that inhibit transformative learning in the classroom, such as rules and sanctions imposed on welfare women returning to work in a family empowerment project (Christopher, Dunnagan, Duncan, and Paul, 2001); the downside of cohort experiences where there is often an unequal distribution of group responsibilities and an emphasis on task completion instead of reflective dialogue (Scribner and Donaldson, 2001); and the need to be deliberate, both by the teachers and program design, for transformative learning to occur in graduate education (Taylor, 2003). Nevertheless, many questions remain about how to foster transformative learning in the classroom.

In response to and almost seven years since the last New Directions issue on transformative learning, there is a need to return to the classroom and look through the lens of those who have engaged in the practice of fostering transformative learning. This volume therefore focuses on how seasoned practitioners and scholars grapple with the fundamental issues associated with transformative learning (for example, emotion, whole-person learning, power, cultural difference, context, teacher authenticity, and spirituality) in a formal classroom setting; it also explores innovations (such as fiction and writing) that enhance the practice of fostering transformative learning and investigates ethical questions that need to be explored and reflected on when practicing transformative learning in the classroom.

The chapters' authors are an incredible cadre of scholars who have not only vast experience in the practice of fostering transformative learning but also deep understanding of its scholarship. They address concerns raised previously and provide some new ways to think about transformative learning and the means to engage this approach to teaching.

Chapter One, by Patricia Cranton, begins with the nexus of transformative learning: the student-teacher relationship. In particular, she examines the necessity of establishing authentic relationships in the classroom when fostering transformative learning. Cranton offers clarity to an often nebulous and slippery concept by framing the discussion within a five-facet model of authenticity. Furthermore, she offers clear strategies for fostering authentic relationships that account for teacher individuality and contextual constraints that often inhibit the teacher's ability to teach authentically.

Chapter Two begins to get at one of the central challenges of fostering transformative learning: how to engage emotions in the classroom. Although this topic is often not talked about and can be viewed as a nuisance by-product of intense critical reflection, John Dirkx moves the discussion of engaging emotions in the classroom to center stage. He brings to the fore that emotion is not the enemy of reason but is instead integral "to the meaning-making process," particularly unconscious ways of knowing.

Chapter Three, by Jackie Davis-Manigaulte, Lyle Yorks, and Elizabeth Kasl, builds on the previous chapter by offering "a conceptual map for practices that link the affective and rational, specifically, practices that tap imaginal and intuitive ways of knowing" in the classroom. Based on case studies of learners' experiences, the authors introduce presentational ways of knowing that include music, art, dance, movement and mime, and drama. These modalities engage both the affective and the cognitive, allowing a holistic approach to transformative learning for both the learners and the teacher.

Chapter Four grapples with one of the most intriguing phenomena recently associated with fostering transformative learning: engaging spirituality in the adult and higher education classroom. Derise Tolliver and Elizabeth Tisdell bring clarity to this elusive topic and, as the previous chapters do, provide real-life examples of expression that reflect adult learners' "meaning making and a sense of wholeness, healing, and the interconnectedness of all things." Furthermore, they do not overlook the evocative nature of spirituality, and they explore the caveats and risks associated when engaging this concept in practice.

Chapter Five engages the practice of fostering transformative learning from an area rarely researched and discussed: transformation practiced among black women educators. Juanita Johnson-Bailey and Mary Alfred offer a frank discussion on the realities of transformative teaching and learning from the margins. "Black women colleagues see transformative learning as the only medium in which we exist, learn, and teach. Since it is the air we breathe, maybe we just take it for granted and don't attend to or claim it sufficiently." It is a transformative practice grounded in an oppositional spirit, with a true appreciation of how sociopolitical dimensions shape the meaning-making process.

In Chapter Six, Dorothy Ettling offers a thoughtful discussion on the issue of ethics and fostering transformative learning. She explores such questions as, What are the responsibilities of educators as they engage in this work? Do teachers have the right to foster change among students when they know that the consequence of change may have a significant impact on their lives? She also discusses ethical competencies in the form of "ethical capacities" that extend beyond the limits of ethics framed by rationality, providing guidance in the everyday practice of transformative learning.

In addition to these chapters on the challenges associated with fostering transformative learning, I have included two that look at recent innovative approaches to transformative learning. Interestingly, both shed light on the use of text as a powerful medium for fostering change in the classroom. In Chapter Seven, Christine Jarvis shares a fascinating "study of how popular romantic fiction was used to transform students' understandings of the ways in which gendered identities are constructed and their perception of the way textual meanings are determined." Jarvis's work involves women returners in the United Kingdom, where transformation through the use of fiction was stimulated by "imaginative events."

Similarly, in Chapter Eight, Adrienne Burk shares her work with an intensive writing program initiated among undergraduate and graduate students at Simon Fraser University in British Columbia, Canada. This program was instituted across disciplines, and profound changes were seen not only in how courses were constructed but, more significantly, in "the faculty themselves as they revisit and rethink their own scholarly identities and pedagogical strategies." Many of the faculty experienced deep epistemological shifts and began to give greater attention to the role of learning and its relationship to teaching.

My hope is that readers of this volume will gain a greater appreciation for the challenges associated with the practice of fostering transformative learning and a recognition of the complexity of practice beyond the application of strategies and techniques, as well as be motivated to explore and take risks in the classroom, always pushing the limits of what is presently known about transformative education.

A great number of people worked with me on this volume. I thank all of the chapter authors, who found the time in their busy schedules to offer such thoughtful and creative chapters on transformative learning. I thank Patti Thompson, a graduate assistant at Penn State Harrisburg in the adult education doctoral program, for terrific editorial assistance and thoughtful ideas in strengthening this volume. I also thank Tom Nesbit, a colleague and friend, for his continued encouragement and support as I worked on this project.

Edward W. Taylor
Editor

References

Christopher, S., Dunnagan, T., Duncan, S. F., and Paul, L. "Education for Self-Support: Evaluating Outcomes Using Transformative Learning Theory." *Family Relations,* 2001, 50(2), 134–142.

Jarvis, C. "Love Changes Everything: The Transformative Potential of Popular Romantic Fiction." *Studies in the Education of Adults,* 1999, 31(2), 109–123.

Mezirow, J., and Associates (eds.). *Learning as Transformation.* San Francisco: Jossey-Bass, 2000.

Quinnan, T. *Adult Students "At-Risk": Culture Bias in Higher Education.* Westport, Conn.: Bergin and Garvey, 1997.

Scribner, J. P., and Donaldson, J. F. "The Dynamics of Group Learning in a Cohort: From Nonlearning to Transformative Learning." *Educational Administration Quarterly,* 2001, 37, 605–638.

Taylor, E. W. "Fostering Transformative Learning in the Adult Education Classroom." *Canadian Journal of the Study of Adult Education,* 2000, 14, 1–28.

Taylor, E. W. "Looking Back Five Years: A Critical Review of Transformative Learning Theory." In *Proceedings for the Fifth International Transformative Learning Conference.* New York: Teachers College, Columbia University, 2003.

EDWARD W. TAYLOR *is associate professor at Penn State University Harrisburg, Middletown, Pennsylvania.*

1

Authentic relationships between teacher and student form a central process in transformative learning in the class-room. Based on research and theory, this chapter provides practical strategies for educators looking to foster authentic relationships.

Fostering Authentic Relationships in the Transformative Classroom

Patricia Cranton

> Actually, on the evaluations they have some piece of paper where you could write comments. I always read them, and sometimes I say, well, they write that you act like a robot, and you have to think, do you really act like a robot? You have to think about that.
>
> Susan, education professor

> I can think that I am doing so great. I am such a great teacher and the students are going, ah, I hope that he retires soon. . . . It is not easy. It's a difficult thing.
>
> Alex, philosophy professor

Fostering transformative learning in the classroom depends to a large extent on establishing meaningful, genuine relationships with students. In a research project where we worked with twenty-two faculty members over three years to learn about their understanding of authentic teaching, the most-often discussed theme was their relationships with students (Cranton and Carusetta, 2004). Although we were not asking participants directly about transformative learning, it became clear that this was what they were doing or hoping to do in their practice. And at the center of that was the teachers' deep concern about and interest in how students saw them, how they saw students, and the nature of their relationships with each other.

NEW DIRECTIONS FOR ADULT AND CONTINUING EDUCATION, no. 109, Spring 2006 © 2006 Wiley Periodicals, Inc.
Published online in Wiley InterScience (www.interscience.wiley.com) • DOI: 10.1002/ace.203

This chapter begins with a brief overview of my own perspective on transformational learning. I then discuss what authenticity in teaching means, emphasizing authentic relationships between teachers and students. I suggest that the development of authenticity is transformative—that as people form and shape their sense of self, they naturally question those values and assumptions they had previously uncritically assimilated. I then provide practical suggestions for fostering authentic relationships in the transformative classroom, based in theory and research and drawing on my own experience and the wealth of experiences shared by the participants in our research project.

Perspective on Transformative Learning

There has been considerable debate in the literature as to whether transformative learning is rational or extrarational, reflective or imaginative, cognitive or emotional, individual or social. Although most of my work has followed Mezirow's (2000) cognitive, reasoned approach to understanding transformation, my interest in Jung's (1971) concept of individuation and my own research on authenticity have led me to bring some of the alternative perspectives together—not to synthesize them in the way of bringing black and white together to make gray, but rather to suggest that they can and should coexist within a holistic perspective (Cranton and Roy, 2003).

By bringing these strands together, I suggest that the central process of transformative learning may be rational, affective, extrarational, or experiential depending on the person engaged in the learning and the context in which it takes place. One person may consciously engage in a self-reflective process, while another may see the journey as an imaginative one. The same individual in one context (the death of a spouse, for example) may experience transformation as an emotional crisis, while in another context (changing jobs, for example) may experience the process as one of quiet reflection. Transformation may be shared when a group works to question social conditions through collective action (such as during a protest against war or government policy) or individual when a person questions and reframes his or her unique beliefs and assumptions (such as when a learner comes to see that there are complex rather than black-and-white points of view on an issue).

Authenticity

In our research on authenticity in teaching, we talked to faculty members at least once each academic term for three years and observed their teaching on at least two occasions. Through the richness of these conversations and people's earnest attempts to understand the meaning of authenticity in their teaching, we derived a five-faceted model of authenticity (Cranton and Carusetta, 2004):

• Having a strong self-awareness of who we are as teachers and as people

New Directions for Adult and Continuing Education • DOI: 10.1002/ace

- Being aware of the characteristics and preferences of learners and others, including how they are the same and different from our own
- Developing a relationship with learners that fosters our own and their ability to be genuine and open
- Being aware of the context and constraints of teaching and how these factors influence what we do and who we are
- Engaging in critical reflection and critical self-reflection on practice so as to be aware of the assumptions and values we hold and where they originate

The third of these points was the one to which our talk always returned. Teachers struggled with how to be themselves in their relationships with students, where to draw the line in caring for their students, how much of their own lives to share, and when to decide that teaching had become counseling. For example, as two faculty members reveal:

> You have to be present for them. The other thing, it never stops because once somebody has opened up to you like that, they trust you, and if you pass them in the hallway and don't say hello, that is not good. You have to be present all the time. [Lee, business professor]

> I do bring myself as a mom sometimes, you know, talk about my kids . . . most moms are teachers, so I do bring myself to class, definitely. I don't check it at the door and become the instructor. I mean, the instructor is me, and I'm not two different people. [Loretta, education professor]

Jarvis (1992) suggests that people are being authentic when they choose to act so as to "foster the growth and development of each other's being" (p. 113). Jarvis sees this as an experimental and creative act where teachers consciously have the goal of helping another person develop. Teachers and students learn together through dialogue, as Freire (1972) advocates, and the result of authentic teaching is that "teachers learn and grow together with their students" (Jarvis, 1992, p. 114).

Development of Authentic Relationships as Transformative Learning

> Making, helping students make fundamental shifts in their perspective and seeing them when they're doing that. Showing students that there are other ways to think about things. . . . I find that most fulfilling and most rewarding.
>
> I think there's a lot of social, emotional, spiritual connections that go on as well. . . . A big piece of that connecting is the synergy that develops from getting to know people . . . depending on the level of connection . . . not only an aware level, but sometimes there's a spiritual presence, so some of those are really powerful experiences. [Joanne, nursing professor]

New Directions for Adult and Continuing Education • DOI: 10.1002/ace

When teachers do not see students as individual people, authentic relationships are not possible. In educational systems and within the culture of institutions, there are often socially constructed notions of what students are like: "students cannot read and write anymore," "today's students are lazy," and "students are only interested in getting jobs." An uncritical acceptance of these social norms leads educators to define the persona of "student" and then use this persona to form rules about how students behave. If the habitual expectations about how students behave are critically questioned, it is possible for teachers to transform their perspective on students until it becomes multifaceted and open to the differences among the human beings who are their learners.

This then extends into how teachers relate to their students. If they see all students as having some set of characteristics and if those characteristics are objectified and out there, they can have difficulty establishing relationships with individuals. There are lines, boundaries, and rules for interacting with the cardboard figures. As the frame of reference for the concept of "student" becomes more open and permeable through transformative learning, students and educators can develop genuine relationships in which the educator makes a difference in the students' lives and feels a difference in his or her own life as well. For example, one faculty member states, "It's being yourself and not trying to fulfill a role of what people might traditionally think of as a teacher or a great sage or some sort of that kind of image" (Alex, philosophy professor).

Strategies for Fostering Authentic and Transformative Relationships

One of the things I find hard about working in an institution is that my temptation is to break, at certain points, institutional guidelines. Not literally but theoretically in terms of teaching things that are not taught. Running classes in a different way. Thinking of the world differently. [Gary, English professor]

There is no reason for me to pretend that I am all wise, because I can't pull it off . . . whatever that style and the tools and techniques that work for me that fit my personality and how I relate to people and the students and experience how they relate to me. And be genuine with answers. [Katherine, science professor]

How do we get there? How do we develop authentic and transformative relationships with our students? For help with this question, I return to the framework derived from our research project: self-awareness, awareness of others, relationships, context, and criticality. Authentic and transformative relationships cannot exist without these ingredients.

Self-Awareness. To enter into an authentic relationship with students, one that has the potential for transformative dialogue, teachers need to have a good understanding of themselves. In *Becoming an Authentic Teacher in*

New Directions for Adult and Continuing Education • DOI: 10.1002/ace

Higher Education (2001), I suggest a variety of exercises for exploring values, significant experiences, psychological type preferences, and teaching style, including the following:

List ten nouns that describe yourself (for example, *teacher, mother, gardener*) and then look for themes that underlie the descriptors. Are they based on relationships with others? Are they based on what you do in your practice? Are they based on interests or beliefs outside of your practice?

List the ten most significant experiences of your life, and examine and discuss the content of the list with a colleague or friend.

Complete psychological preference inventories such as the PET Type Check (Cranton and Knoop, 1995) or the Myers-Briggs Type Indicator.

Write an autobiography, and then share and discuss the narrative with a colleague or friend.

Create an art or craft piece (painting, collage, sculpture, quilt) to represent who you are.

Such activities may be completed by students as well as by the educator if the content of the course or program is conducive to the integration of self-awareness exploration.

Awareness of Others. In addition to teacher self-awareness, educators need to come to know their students as individuals. Thinking about "the group" or "the class" and characterizing it in some way (a good group, a talkative class, and so forth) is helpful to some extent, but does not provide the kind of knowledge teachers need to form authentic relationships. There are many simple strategies that can be used to get to know students individually:

Before or after class or during breaks in class, chat with people about their families, interests, and background.

Have students write on an index card their reasons for taking a course or their special interests in relation to the course.

Get to know people's learning styles either through a formal survey (for example, Kolb's Learning Style Inventory (Kolb, 1984) or by asking informal questions about how people prefer to learn.

Ask for frequent feedback from students.

Incorporate an online component into the course, and encourage participants to write about their reactions to discussions, readings, and class activities.

Relationships. Different teachers have different preferences for the nature of the relationships they like to establish with students. To be authentic and develop authentic relationships, it is important that teachers not contradict their values or their philosophy of teaching in this respect. Elsewhere, I have described three kinds of teacher-student relationships, though it is obviously more complex than this (Cranton, 2003). Educators may form relationships based on a respectful distance, collegiality, or closeness. When respectful distance is the basis of knowing students, the relationship occurs primarily through the subject area and focuses on the learning. In collegial relationships, the educator views the learner as a future or a current colleague, works collaboratively, and engages in mutual sharing of experience and expertise. In a close relationship, teachers and students come to know each other as people both inside and outside the classroom. Each style of relationship is equally likely to encourage transformative learning, but educators must find the way that is comfortable for them and congruent with their values, beliefs, and philosophy of teaching. I question the extent to which deep shifts in the way in which people understand the world can occur in relationships based on personas or stereotypes. I provide some illustrations, which may give guidance for the person seeking more authentic relationships.

In my first interview with Katherine for our research project, she told me that she loved her students and laughed a little with embarrassment. As I got to know Katherine better, I came to understand what she meant and how authentic her relationships with her students were. Students felt free to come into Katherine's office at any time, including during our interviews, and she always welcomed them and demonstrated an enthusiastic interest in whatever they had to say. But the way Katherine connected with her students was on a deeper level than that. She would call students at home who had not come to class to check whether they were all right; she would arrange day care and travel; she would invite students who were away from home to join her family for a Thanksgiving meal. Katherine joked about being a "mother duck" with a trail of baby ducks behind her, and indeed, there was a strong maternal nurturance in the way she took care of her students. Katherine's transformative goal as a science teacher is to foster a change in students' perception of science, especially among the young women in her class.

I met Bob in summer school where I regularly teach a course on methods and strategies in adult education for new college instructors. Bob teaches in the trades; his students are almost always men. Bob sees himself as working with "colleagues in training." He works alongside his students in the shop, draws on their experiences in the field, and shares his own experiences. There is a lot of laughter in his classroom and in his shop as people share stories about their trade, tell jokes, and complain in a good-natured kind of way about the fast-changing technology in the trade. Bob often joins his students at the pub after class and maintains a camaraderie that is typical of the workplace. His transformative goals in his teaching are to help students see that relationships with the owners of the cars are as important as the technical skills they use in repairing the cars, and that critical and innovative thinking about their work is essential in a trade that changes daily.

Tang-Mei teaches instructional technology, and I met her in an online teaching environment. Although she has been in North America for a few years, Tang-Mei's Chinese culture plays a strong role in her perception of relationships with students. She is no longer the directive and in-control teacher she was before she began studying adult education, but she believes strongly in establishing a professional, respectful relationship where students and teacher trust and like each other but do not share personal stories or go to each other for emotional support. Tang-Mei explained to me that she sees that kind of relationship as belonging with friends and family, not with students. She honors her students' concerns about the subject area and their questions about learning, and she always listens carefully and quietly when a student comes to her office to discuss the course. She says that her students do not come to her with personal problems, which I first found to be curious, but later came to understand as something that Tang-Mei consciously and subtly sets up from the first day of class. Tang-Mei's transformative goals include helping students to question the premises underlying the use of technology in education.

Context. Educators delineate several kinds of constraints to their ability to be authentic in their teaching—mandatory curriculum, grading policies, class sizes, availability of resources, departmental or institutional expectations, and social norms about the role of teachers (Cranton and Carusetta, 2004). Not all of these constraints directly affect relationships with students, though in one sense, anything that influences a teacher's authenticity also influences her relationships.

Shannon is a college teacher of graphic design who participated in my summer school course. One day she asked the class for advice on a situation from her teaching the previous year. In her program, students have an extended workplace practicum where they spend time in the field and come back and present what they have learned to their classmates. One of Shannon's students had given a poor presentation and had therefore failed the entire practicum. Shannon was appalled, and she tried to intervene on behalf of the student, arguing that he should be able to repeat the presentation only rather than the entire practicum. Shannon came up against departmental policy that prevented this and felt she had damaged not only her relationship with this student but with others who relied on her help in making their way through the practicum.

I list some strategies for dealing with constraints that influence a teacher's ability to establish authentic relationships:

Become familiar with written and unwritten policies and procedures, and question those that seem to have the potential of interfering with good relationships.

Find out how policies are established, and become a part of the policymaking procedures.

Discuss institutional norms and expectations with colleagues; have a critical voice in questioning those norms.

See yourself as an advocate for students rather than an enforcer of institutional rules.

New Directions for Adult and Continuing Education • DOI: 10.1002/ace

Be open with students about the policies and social norms that influence or inhibit your practice.

Critical Reflection. Critical reflection is a central process in Mezirow's (2000) conceptualization of transformative learning. My own understanding of transformative learning has expanded to include extrarational and affective processes (Cranton and Roy, 2003), but critical reflection as it is traditionally defined remained important in our research participants' descriptions of authenticity in teaching (Cranton and Carusetta, 2004). In order to develop authenticity, educators felt that they needed to distinguish their sense of self as a teacher from the collective persona of teacher, and that calls for critical reflection on the assumptions and values of practice. There is little authenticity in running with the herd. I believe that extracting oneself from the herd can also be an intuitive, imaginative, and affective process, but perhaps because of the pervasiveness of the educational social norm about the importance of critical reflection itself, most people spoke in those terms. In my suggestions here, I incorporate some ideas that go beyond rational critical reflection and I focus on those activities that are especially relevant to fostering authentic relationships:

Keep a teaching journal in which you focus on and critically examine the nature of your relationships with students.
Set up a blog (Web-based dialogue) with colleagues who share your interest in understanding and promoting good relationships with students.
Create a collage, make a painting, or write a poem to represent your feelings about your students.
Follow Dirkx's (2000) advice to pay attention to the everyday occurrences in the classroom, and use an imaginative process to recognize, name, and understand those happenings.
Talk to students about their perceptions of and feelings about the events and interactions in the classroom.

Conclusion

Although transformative learning is stimulated by any event or experience that calls into question our habitual expectations about ourselves and the world around us, in the context of the classroom, it likely depends on the nature of dialogue and relationships between teacher and student and among students. Students receiving information from an authority figure whom they do not know as a person can easily accept or disregard that information. But when a person is engaged in a serious dialogue with someone he or she knows, likes, and trusts, the potential for the examination of previously uncritically absorbed values and assumptions is, I suggest, much greater.

Authenticity in teaching has to do with self-awareness, awareness of others, relationships, context, and leading a critical life. Fostering authentic relationships has something to do with each of these five facets of authenticity. Only in popular psychology self-help books can we find series of steps to follow to develop good relationships. I believe that through conscious and deliberate consideration of who we are as human beings, we can find the path that will lead us to authentic relationships with others.

References

Cranton, P. *Becoming an Authentic Teacher in Higher Education.* Malabar, Fla.: Krieger, 2001.

Cranton, P. *Finding Our Way: A Guide for Adult Educators.* Toronto: Wall & Emerson, 2003.

Cranton, P., and Carusetta, E. "Perspectives on Authenticity." *Adult Education Quarterly,* 2004, *55*(1), 5–22.

Cranton, P., and Knoop, R. "Assessing Psychological Type: The PET Type Check." *General, Social, and Genetic Psychological Monographs,* 1995, *121*(2), 247–274. www.vitalknowledge.com/highereducation.

Cranton, P., and Roy, M. "When the Bottom Falls Out of the Bucket: A Holistic Perspective on Transformative Learning." *Journal of Transformative Education,* 2003, *1*(2), 86–98.

Dirkx, J. "After the Burning Bush: Transformative Learning as Imaginative Engagement with Everyday Experience." In C. Wiessner, S. Meyer, and D. Fuller (eds.), *Challenges of Practice: Transformative Learning in Action. The Proceedings of the Third International Conference on Transformative Learning.* New York: Teachers College, Columbia University, 2000.

Freire, P. *Pedagogy of the Oppressed.* Harmondsworth, England: Penguin Books, 1972.

Jarvis, P. *Paradoxes of Learning: On Becoming an Individual in Society.* San Francisco: Jossey-Bass, 1992.

Jung, C. *Psychological Types.* Princeton, N.J.: Princeton University Press, 1971. (Originally published 1921.)

Kolb, D. *Experiential Learning: Experience as a Source of Learning and Development.* Upper Saddle River, N.J.: Prentice Hall, 1984.

Mezirow, J. "Learning to Think Like an Adult: Core Concepts of Transformation Theory." In J. Mezirow and Associates (eds.), *Learning as Transformation: Critical Perspectives on a Theory in Progress.* San Francisco: Jossey-Bass, 2000.

PATRICIA CRANTON is visiting professor at Penn State University Harrisburg, Middletown, Pennsylvania.

2

Emotion-laden images that arise within adult learning provide a symbolic language for helping teachers and learners understand and facilitate transformation at both the individual and group levels.

Engaging Emotions in Adult Learning: A Jungian Perspective on Emotion and Transformative Learning

John M. Dirkx

Susan, a student in a community-based adult education program, was preparing to take the writing portion of the exam for her general equivalency diploma. A middle-aged, single mother of two, she was asked by her teacher to complete a written practice essay as a way to help gauge her readiness to take the exam. After a time, Susan finished this task and turned in the work to her teacher. As she began to review the essay, the teacher was shocked to realize that she was reading Susan's will. When she asked Susan about this, Susan told her she was afraid that her ex-husband would kill her and she wanted her children protected.

Following a three-hour workshop for community college faculty on generational differences in teaching and learning, James, a seasoned teacher of twenty years, approached the facilitator to thank him for the session and to share with him his reactions. In an excited voice, James conveyed that the content had provided him with insights into some differences among the students with whom we worked. "In addition," he said as his voice lowered to a more introspective and contemplative tone and his eyes grew moist, "I had some 'aha' moments about my relationships with my own teenage sons and my own father."

These brief vignettes illustrate the powerful emotional context in which much of adult learning occurs. Affective issues influence why adults show up for educational programs, their interest in the subject matter, and the processes by which they engage the material, their experiences, the teacher, and one

NEW DIRECTIONS FOR ADULT AND CONTINUING EDUCATION, no. 109, Spring 2006 © 2006 Wiley Periodicals, Inc.
Published online in Wiley InterScience (www.interscience.wiley.com) • DOI: 10.1002/ace.204

another. While these emotional issues are usually manifest in an explicit manner, they often reflect dynamics that are more subtle, implicit, and even beyond conscious awareness (Salzberger-Wittenberg, Henry, and Osborne, 1983).

How can we as adult educators make sense of these expressions of affect to which adult learners such as Susan and James give voice? What do they say, if anything, about the process of learning and its potential for fostering transformative change? Prevailing views often regard their manifestation as a potential disruption of the learning experience, a need that has to be addressed before actual learning can take place, or a potential for motivating students to learn. Ruggiero (2003) speaks for many educators when he says, "Even a brief reflection on everyday experience will reveal several negative characteristics of feelings" (p. xxii). While research is increasingly demonstrating that emotion is not the enemy of reason (Imel, 2003), as Ruggiero suggests, relatively few scholars and practitioners in adult and higher education regard emotion as integral to the meaning-making process and as demonstrative of underlying and largely unconscious forms of meaning associated with learning.

In this chapter, I suggest that the expression of affective and emotionally laden issues often reveals the ways and forms through which adult learners give voice to unconscious personal meaning of their learning experiences (Chodorow, 1999). Using the theoretical framework of depth psychology (Davis, 2003), I explore how we as educators might learn to use the idea of emotion-laden images (Dirkx, 2001a) as a means of helping learners working through unconscious psychic conflicts and dilemmas associated with the learning task or content, and of fostering opportunities among our learners for meaning making, deep change, and transformation.

Emotions and Feelings as Expression of Unconscious Meaning in Adult Learning

The scholarly literature reflects how the experience of emotion is intimately bound up with and central to what it means to be human (Lupton, 1998). Yet in education, we demonstrate a checkered engagement with the affective dimension of learning. Our forty-year love affair with Bloom's taxonomy includes an explicit but ambivalent recognition of an "affective domain" of instructional objectives, but, as Rompelman (2002) suggests, "The impact of this domain is often overlooked or misunderstood" (p. 1). In the 1960s, Richard Jones (1968) challenged us to think about the feelings and fantasies that students bring to the learning experience and how we might more fully integrate these aspects of their lives in our teaching. But as scholars and practitioners became increasingly enamored with the cognitive and intellectual dimensions of teaching and learning, such seminal voices on affective learning receded. A scholarship of emotion in teaching and learning, however, is now again emerging (Britzman, 1998; Dirkx, 2001b). Goleman's (1995) introduction of emotional intelligence, while controversial and appropriately contested, at least moved consideration of emotion from the margins of educational discourse.

Much of adult learning theory already implicitly incorporates or recognizes the affective dimension in the learning process (Imel, 2003), and recent work continues to explore the affective, emotional, and spiritual dimensions of adult learning, development, and transformation (Dirkx, 2000, 2001b; Fenwick, 2003; Heron, 1992; Kegan, 2000; Palmer, 1993; Taylor, 2001). These approaches to affect and emotion in adult learning provide various ways of understanding how emotions reveal aspects of a learner's perceived reality.

One approach is to think of a learner's emotions in a transparent or literal manner, as windows that reveal experienced realities. For example, a student's anger at the instructor might be interpreted literally as being unhappy and dissatisfied with the instructional methods being used, prompting us to try to find alternative methods that more effectively address her needs or more clearly justify our current methods.

But we might also interpret this anger more symbolically, as standing for a deeper, underlying personal or transpersonal issue that has been evoked by the instructional processes. This student's anger might be expressing feelings of being overwhelmed by her group, of not having a voice or sense of identity in the group. Depending on which perspective we take, we will adopt quite different pedagogical strategies to address the anger with instructional process. The workshop on generational differences that James attended suggests that the meaning of this topic for him is intimately bound up with relationship issues.

Here our gaze is drawn to the experience and manifestation of emotional dynamics in learning. These dynamics suggest largely unconscious issues evoked by various aspects of the learning setting, such as the self, designated leaders, other learners, the context in which learning occurs, and the task that is the explicit focus of our learning. In his discussion of a Jungian perspective on transformative learning, Boyd (1991) refers to the unconscious emotional issues evoked within individual learners as psychic dilemmas, "a semi-conscious discord—an unresolved conflict that the individual is generally able to acknowledge with prodding or encouragement. . . . A person experiencing a psychic dilemma is confronted with two opposing choices" (pp. 179–180). The experience of this dilemma is often experienced as a draining away of psychic energy, while its resolution through conscious realization and reworking is often accompanied by deeper insights into the self and a renewed sense of energy and life.

Unconscious emotional dynamics may contribute to resistance to learning itself (Britzman, 1998), as well as the emergence of new levels of awareness of the self-in-relation-to-others (Boyd, 1991). In the opening vignettes, attention only to the surface, manifest content of these emotions may contribute to misinterpretation or incomplete understanding of underlying meaning that is actually influencing and shaping the learner's classroom behaviors. Using Jungian theory can help us identify and understand the powerful role that emotions and unconscious dynamics potentially play in the transformative dimensions of adult learning.

Emotion-Laden Images in Adult Learning

So far I have argued that within adult learning, we need to consider the symbolic meaning of emotion and affect. I have suggested that such expression suggests a possible connection between a learner's unconscious psychic conflict or dilemma and some aspect of the learning experience. In this section, I explain how emotion-laden images mediate a conscious relationship with unconscious contents of our psyches.

Jungian perspectives on emotion in learning differ sharply from more traditional and dominant Freudian views of the emotions in learning, which generally characterize them as personal pathologies that need to be resolved. Dominant perspectives regard them as "hang-ups" or "psychic distortions" (Mezirow, 1991), disrupting the learning process and our capacity to adapt to the demands of our outer reality. To function effectively with others, we need to attend to and work through these potentially debilitating emotional issues.

Jungian scholars, however, tend to understand many of the powerful emotional issues that arise within the learning environment, at least in part, as intrinsic aspects of being human (Boyd, 1991; Dirkx, 2000; Scott, forthcoming). Their expression is bound up with what Jung (1969) refers to as individuation, a process by which we come to recognize and develop an awareness of who we are and how we relate to others. As a result of the work of individuation, each person comes to a deeper understanding, realization, and appreciation of who he or she is apart from the pressures of the social and cultural contexts in which they are inextricably embedded (Jacobi, 1967). It is only through this process of individuation that we can develop more authentic relationships with others and with ourselves.

The process of individuation is mediated largely through emotion-laden images. As they are being used here, images refer to affective, imaginative, and unconsciously created representations of our experience that arise spontaneously in awareness. We are usually not fully conscious of the presence of these images, which often have the shape and consistency of dream images, in our awareness (Watkins, 1984). Like dream images, these waking images are largely beyond our conscious, rational control. For example, the structure of learning environments often evokes powerful emotions among adult students. Increasing anger among some students may cluster around the complaint that there is too little structure and guidance provided. Others, however, may feel deauthorized and limited by too much structure. In this example, learning structure represents an emotion-laden image that is probably conveying deeper, underlying issues within the setting, such as a need for or fear of dependence on strong, external authority

New Directions for Adult and Continuing Education • DOI: 10.1002/ace

figures. Before they even become conscious of it, learners often quickly find themselves in the grip of powerful emotional dynamics related to this issue.

Unconsciously, images are often experienced as the manifestation of compulsions, obsessions, or complexes, taking over our conscious awareness (Singer, 1994). The common phrase "pushing my buttons" reflects the way our conscious selves can be overtaken by these powerful unconscious emotions ("my buttons"). Given the appropriate conditions, however, we can enter into a conscious relationship with these images. Such work may reveal how aspects of ourselves are being expressed through these emotion-laden images. My resistance to structure within the learning environment may be an expression of my own deep fears of being too dependent on others. By embracing their manifestation in images that populate our everyday interactions with others, we reclaim these projected emotions as our own. Conscious participation in this process directs our psychic energy toward creative, life-enhancing, constructive, and potentially transformative activities.

Through this ongoing journey, we learn to become more fully who we are as persons, which enables us to more fully and authentically enter into relationships with others and the world (Cranton, 2001). Without such a conscious relationship with these dynamic forces, our lives are less meaningful. We may even experience their potentially destructive force in the form of personal pathologies such as obsessions, compulsions, addictions, depression, or other forms of an essentially divided life (Palmer, 2004). When we take seriously the responsibility of developing a more conscious relationship with the unconscious dimensions of our being, we enter into a profoundly transformative, life-changing process.

Emotion-Laden Images and Transformative Learning

Since Mezirow's (1975) early work on perspective transformation, additional research has suggested that transformative learning involves the self in an intense process of meaning making that reflects the person's relationship with both the self and his or her sociocultural context (Taylor, 1998). While at once personal, it is also deeply social and engages the learner in collaborative relationships with others. This research suggests that developing awareness of these relationships involves cognitive, affective, somatic, and spiritual processes, mediated by reflective analysis, story, symbol, or ritual. Such work may lead to profound shifts in one's awareness or consciousness of being in the world—what we refer to as transformative learning.

Emotions are deeply involved in the process of transformative learning in at least two fundamental ways. First, the process of critical reflection, as described by Mezirow as central to transformative learning, essentially calls into question and invites exploration of alternative ways of being-in-the-world. As learners make explicit and reflect on their assumptions, the process may be accompanied by various emotions, such as guilt, fear, shame, a sense of loss, or general anxiety. For example, coming to grips with racist or sexist assumptions we may be holding about our world may be associated with powerful feelings about ourselves or our past actions. Second, a person's unconscious emotional responses to various aspects of the learning experience can serve as an expression of the journey of individuation, an area of one's psychic life seeking voice within a particular context. The opening vignettes represent examples of the latter.

In either case, I argue that expression of such powerful emotions within the learning experience suggests deep involvement of the learner's psyche or self. To understand and work with these emotions, we need a kind of language to develop a conscious dialogue and relationship with those aspects of the psyche expressed through these emotions. The language and processes of critical reflection (Mezirow, 1991) do not seem well suited to working with these extrarational, unconscious processes and dynamics. The main way we work with unconscious psychic content is through the language of the imagination, expressed through images (Moore, 1992; Sells, 2000; Watkins, 1984). Once we become familiar with this language, we begin to see beyond a learner's literal concerns to underlying and deeply emotional issues. For example, the presence of doctoral students among a master's-level graduate course may evoke among the less experienced participants unconscious feelings of inferiority and inability to compete. Dimly perceived feelings of mistrust or fear of not being accepted may be reflected in a student's timid and reluctant participation in group discussion. Analysis of the role of the mother image in group process may evoke unresolved issues with a learner's own mother and cause him to break down and leave the room. Each of these examples may be understood as deep, underlying emotional issues evoked by various aspects of the learning experience. They reflect the ways we construct and reconstruct the meaning of our experiences and our sense of self and how we work through the psychic dilemmas that are often associated with the movement and journey of the self.

Engaging emotion-laden images within the learning experience in an imaginative rather than a literal way helps facilitate the movement of individuation by attending to the unconscious meaning-making processes at work within the human psyche. As such, it contributes to powerful processes of transformation. In the next section, we explore how we as educators might use these images to help foster transformative learning.

Using Emotion-Laden Images to Facilitate Transformative Learning

In formal adult learning settings that are interactive and dialogical, the unconscious is often expressed through emotionally laden experiences, images, and relationships. These contexts are locations for the work represented by transformative learning: (1) learning to recognize our processes of individuation, that is, the expression and movement of our personal myths (Bond, 1993) as they are manifest within formal settings of adult learning; and (2) developing a more conscious relationship with their expression in our lives. Central to this process in formal settings of adult learning is developing awareness of emotion-laden images that are evoked and animated by and associated with our interactions and relationships with others in the setting, as well as the content being studied.

Instructors can use the group process to help facilitate this approach to transformative learning. In a graduate seminar that I teach, a small group of students had been meeting for several weeks when the group process seemed to bog down. Their interactions were marked by increased disagreements and sharp emotional outbursts, and several members complained that it felt as if they were getting nowhere. To help them develop a deeper awareness of the issues, I asked them for our next session to engage in a kind of active imagination activity (Chodorow, 1997). There are various ways to use active imagination to develop a conscious dialogue with unconscious material (Watkins, 2000), but I suggested a brief writing project. I asked each of them to find some quiet time and a comfortable location and to relax before beginning. Then I instructed them to give the group a name (not using any of the names of the group members) and engage for approximately twenty minutes in an imagined dialogue with this group person through writing. I asked them not to think about what they were writing but simply to engage in this imagined conversation with the group person and to record in writing what was said. Following the dialogue, I asked them to reflect on how they felt during the process and then afterward. At our next meeting, several group members reported that this experience had been powerful in helping them get in touch with issues that were part of their experience in this group. Although not all disclosed their dialogues, enough did to help move the group through the impasse in which it seemed to be stuck.

In a well-documented case analysis, Boyd (1991) illustrates how the context of group relations and dynamics facilitates a developing awareness for one group member of what Boyd refers to as a "psychic dilemma." For Mary, the focus of Boyd's analysis, the dilemma involved unresolved issues with her mother that were being mirrored and played out in the context of her interactions with the group. At first, Mary's interactions with the group contributed to a growing distance between her and other group members, as well as a sense of stuckness within the group as a whole. As she and the group became increasingly aware of the content of these interactions, energy returned to their exchanges, and the group once again became more animated. In concluding his analysis of Mary, Boyd observed, "There was ample evidence that Mary projected aspects of her dilemma into the social system of the group, as well as onto certain members of the group" (p. 201). Through the use of appropriately timed metaphors and analogies, the leader gently kept the issue of Mary's relationship and interactions with the group in front of them. This facilitation allowed Mary and the group to work through these issues in ways that were transformative to both her and the group's development.

New Directions for Adult and Continuing Education • DOI: 10.1002/ace

Finally, adult educators can also foster transformative learning through work with images by the use of readings or text material. Jane (not her real name) was a member of a group of eight graduate students enrolled in an advanced seminar on teaching and learning in higher and adult education. The seminar had been meeting weekly for several weeks when, in response to an assigned article on the labyrinth (Compton, 2002), Jane posted this observation to the class Web site:

> The reading for this week about the labyrinth took me quite a while to read because I'd had a very powerful, I would say transformative, experience walking a labyrinth in mid-September of this year. . . . It's hard for me to articulate the experience because I can't find the words to fully describe it. Words just come up short. This was maybe my third time walking a labyrinth, but this was the first time I felt transformed as opposed to just calmed. . . . I may get a bit teary eyed. I don't experience these tears as sadness, but more as a reflection of the intensity of the experience.

This excerpt clearly shows how emotional experiences are associated with images that arise within assigned texts and how these images foster deeper engagement of the self with the learning process.

The expression and experience of emotion within the learning experience provide an opportunity for establishing a dialogue with those unconscious aspects of ourselves seeking expression through various images, feelings, and behaviors within the learning setting. As some of the preceding examples have illustrated, the expression of powerful affect or emotion, associated with particular instructional content or processes in adult learning, usually suggests there is more to the experience than meets the eye.

To sense this dimension of the learning experience, I usually listen to my own reaction to a student or group interaction. Affectively laden issues involve me as the instructor as well, and I often sense their presence by a tightening in my stomach or an increased sense of anxiety. Often in such situations, instructors might feel attacked, such as when students complain about the instructional process, or their grades, or the overwhelming nature of the assignments. But we want to avoid responding defensively to such situations. We should interpret such comments in a symbolic rather than a personal way. We should seek to create within the learning environment a safe container for these emotions—one in which the learner feels held but not held onto, contained but not constrained. By helping the student elaborate the story or narrative surrounding his or her issues, rather than analyzing or seeking justification for their reactions, we can further the imaginative work necessary for transformation.

For Jane, the assigned reading evoked emotions associated with walking the labyrinth. The text opened a doorway to some deeper hidden emotions in her life, some of which she did not particularly like (the possibility that something hidden represents something dark). The experience seemed

New Directions for Adult and Continuing Education • DOI: 10.1002/ace

to be "uncovering something hidden" or unconscious, underscoring the central and critical importance of the unconscious in meaning making and transformative learning. Jane's experience demonstrates how an image within an assigned reading evoked for her an intensely emotional experience. She understood this reaction to the text as arising from an earlier experience with the image, and that pointed to particular aspects of her journey as a doctoral student. Jung characterized this changing relationship as a process of individuation. As Jane reflects in her story, "I would describe it as uncovering something hidden." She feels less driven by a sense of obligation or what others expect of her and more by a deeper sense of her own inner being, which her experience of the labyrinth has helped her recognize and become aware. The narrative nature of the course and our attention to experience allowed her to feel safe enough to share this experience with the rest of the group.

In the case of Mary, becoming aware of how her intrapersonal issues were played out and made visible in her interactions with fellow group members provided her with the first steps in her long journey of change and personal transformation. The instructor provides this guidance not through literal interpretations and analysis but through metaphors and parable-like stories that allow her and the group to connect in an imaginative way, rather than intellectually, with the emotional issues represented in this process. As she develops awareness and becomes conscious of these projections, she is able to own them as part of her personality. She can then develop ways that provide her the means to gradually outgrow the psychic dilemma she was experiencing within the small learning group. This process reflects transformation in the Jungian sense—"change in the deepest sense of the word, a form of rebirth" (Boyd, 1991, p. 179).

These vignettes show that adult learners often find that something they have experienced in their interactions with others in the learning setting or have read as part of their learning experience evokes within them powerful emotional reactions. Transformative learning is often characterized by such intense, emotionally laden experiences that are mediated by powerful but often dimly perceived images. Like dreams, the experience of these images cannot be fully articulated through words. As Lupton (1998) suggests, "Emotions are often felt or experienced at the unconscious rather than the conscious level of experience. Emotions may be expressed in dreams or fantasies rather than put into discourse, and thus may at times be 'extra-discursive' as well as 'extra-rational'" (p. 28). Emotion-laden images that come to populate the learner's conscious awareness reflect these unconscious meaning-making processes.

Yet the experience and its associated learning illustrated in the previous vignettes are as real to the participants as any intellectual achievement or mastery of particular content areas. Similar work may be fostered through the selective use of fiction, poetry, and movies related to the overall focus of the learning group. Asking learners to maintain a personal journal related to their use of these curricular materials provides them with an opportunity to make explicit the emotion-laden images evoked by the material and to reflect on and even engage in dialogue with aspects of these images.

I also ask learners to use free-writing as an aspect of their journal work. In this process, the students initially focus on a powerful image or symbol from our group meeting or that arose within their readings. I then ask them to create a quiet space for their journaling, set out a given period of time (say, ten minutes), and then recall this image within their mind's eye. As the image comes into focus, I instruct them to record whatever enters their consciousness and not to stop writing for the duration of the allotted time. I also periodically ask them to reflect more consciously on several of these entries at a time and observe patterns or themes that may be evident within the free-writing entries. This process allows them to connect more fully with the powerful images arising within their learning experiences and begin to integrate them within a more conscious understanding of what these images and the learning experience in general means to them.

Adult learning experiences are populated with such unconscious images that reflect our emotional investment in ourselves and our relationships with the world. Working with these emotion-laden images contributes to transformative learning by deepening both the meaning of what we are studying and what it means to us in the course of our lives.

Conclusion

Almost thirty years ago, Jack Mezirow (1975) initiated a conversation and way of thinking about adult learning that has become one of the most generative lines of scholarship in the field. Since this seminal work, many others have contributed to the development of a more nuanced and comprehensive perspective on transformative learning. While Mezirow (1991) provides an essentially cognitive frame for thinking about transformative learning, Robert Boyd (Boyd and Myers, 1988) introduced the field to the use of Jungian theory as a way of understanding the affective, expressive, and spiritual dimensions of this form of adult learning. The scholarship of transformative learning has essentially evolved along these two broad lines of inquiry, with these seminal thinkers and their research serving as pillars for a more integrated understanding of how adults use the contexts of their formal learning experiences to construct and reconstruct personal meaning.

Increasingly in these settings, imaginative approaches to emotion and affect are beginning to supplement reliance on critical reflection and analysis as a means of furthering deep and potentially transformative experiences. These approaches do not displace or minimize the very real fear that formal learning experiences may evoke in individuals about spousal abuse, or their deep dissatisfaction with group learning, or a sense of regret, melancholy, and lost opportunities associated with personal relationships with signifi-

New Directions for Adult and Continuing Education • DOI: 10.1002/ace

cant others. Rather, they provide a way of thinking more symbolically about the expression of emotional issues among adult learners and how these issues might reflect the powerful movement and journey of souls, a journey that is at once both deeply rooted in the here-and-now and in ageless myths and that is personal and transpersonal—a journey that mirrors both the contexts of one's individual biography and the culture of the moment. Understanding the complexities of these intersecting dynamics, dimensions, and movements is the challenge for those seeking to understand the transformative potential of adult learning.

References

Bond, D. S. *Living Myth: Personal Meaning as a Way of Life*. Boston: Shambhala, 1993.

Boyd, R. D. "Mary: A Case Study of Personal Transformation in a Small Group." In R. D. Boyd (ed.), *Personal Transformations in Small Groups: A Jungian Perspective*. London: Routledge, 1991.

Boyd, R. D., and Myers, J. G. "Transformative Education." *International Journal of Lifelong Education,* 1988, 7(4), 261–284.

Britzman, D. P. *Lost Subjects, Contested Objects: Toward a Psychoanalytic Inquiry of Learning*. Albany, N.Y.: SUNY Press, 1998.

Chodorow, J. (ed.). *Jung on Active Imagination*. Princeton, N.J.: Princeton University Press, 1997.

Chodorow, N. J. *The Power of Feelings: Personal Meaning in Psychoanalysis, Gender, and Culture*. New Haven, Conn.: Yale University Press, 1999.

Compton, V. "The Labyrinth: Site and Symbol of Transformation." In E. V. O'Sullivan, A. Morrel, and M. A. O'Connor (eds.), *Expanding the Boundaries of Transformative Learning: Essays on Theory and Praxis*. New York: Palgrave, 2002.

Cranton, P. *Becoming an Authentic Teacher in Higher Education*. Malabar, Fla.: Krieger, 2001.

Davis, R. H. *Jung, Freud, and Hillman: Three Depth Psychologies in Context*. Westport, Conn.: Praeger, 2003.

Dirkx J. M. "Transformative Learning and the Journey of Individuation." *ERIC Digest,* 2000, no. 223. (ED 448 305)

Dirkx, J. M. "Images, Transformative Learning, and the Work of Soul." *Adult Learning,* 2001a, 12(3), 15–16.

Dirkx, J. M. "The Power of Feeling: Emotion, Imagination, and the Construction of Meaning in Adult Learning." In S. B. Merriam (ed.), *The New Update on Adult Learning Theory*. San Francisco: Jossey-Bass, 2001b.

Fenwick, T. J. *Learning Through Experience: Troubling Orthodoxies and Intersecting Questions*. Malabar, FL: Krieger, 2003.

Goleman, D. *Emotional Intelligence*. New York: Bantam, 1995.

Heron, J. *Feeling and Personhood: Psychology in Another Key*. Thousand Oaks, Calif.: Sage, 1992.

Imel, S. *Effect of Emotions on Learning in Adult, Career, and Career-Technical Education*. ERIC Trends and Issues Alert, Document No. 43, 2003.

Jacobi, J. *The Way of Individuation*. New York: Harcourt Brace, 1967.

Jones, R. M. *Fantasy and Feeling in Education*. New York: HarperCollins, 1968.

Jung, C. G. *The Archetypes and the Collective Unconscious*. Collected Works of C. G. Jung, Vol. 9, Pt. 1. Princeton, N.J.: Princeton University Press, 1969.

Kegan, R. "What Form Transforms? A Constructive Developmental Approach to Transformative Learning." In J. Mezirow and Associates (eds.), *Learning as Transformation: Critical Perspectives on a Theory in Progress*. San Francisco: Jossey-Bass, 2000.

Lupton, D. *The Emotional Self: A Sociocultural Explanation.* Thousand Oaks, Calif.: Sage, 1998.

Mezirow, J. *Education for Perspective Transformation: Women's Re-Entry Programs in Community Colleges.* New York: Center for Adult Education, Teachers College, Columbia University, 1975.

Mezirow, J. *Transformative Dimensions of Adult Learning.* San Francisco: Jossey-Bass, 1991.

Moore, T. *Care of the Soul: A Guide for Cultivating Depth and Sacredness in Everyday Life.* New York: HarperCollins, 1992.

Palmer, P. J. *To Know as We Are Known: Education as a Spiritual Journey.* San Francisco: HarperSanFrancisco, 1993.

Palmer, P. J. *Hidden Wholeness: The Journey Toward an Undivided Life: Welcoming the Soul and Weaving Community.* San Francisco: Jossey-Bass, 2004.

Rompelman, L. *Affective Teaching.* Lanham, Md.: University Press of America, 2002.

Ruggiero, V. R. *Making your Mind Matter: Strategies for Increasing Practical Intelligence.* Lanham, Md.: Rowman & Littlefield, 2003.

Salzberger-Wittenberg, I., Henry, G., and Osborne, E. *The Emotional Experience of Learning and Teaching.* London: Routledge, 1983.

Scott, S. A. "Way of Seeing: Transformation for a New Century." In T. Fenwick, T. Nesbit, and B. Spencer (eds.), *Learning for Life: Canadian Readings in Adult Education.* (2nd ed.) Toronto: Thompson Educational Publishing, forthcoming.

Sells, B. (ed.). *Working with Images: The Theoretical Base of Archetypal Psychology.* Woodstock, Conn.: Spring Publications, 2000.

Singer, J. *Boundaries of the Soul: The Practice of Jung's Psychology.* New York: Doubleday, 1994.

Taylor, E. W. *The Theory and Practice of Transformative Learning: A Critical Review.* Information Series, no. 374. Columbus, Ohio: ERIC Clearinghouse on Adult, Career and Vocational Education, 1998.

Taylor, E. W. "Transformative Learning: A Neurobiological Perspective of the Role of Emotions and Unconscious Ways of Knowing." *International Journal of Lifelong Learning,* 2001, *20,* 218–236.

Watkins, M. *Waking Dreams.* (3rd ed.) Woodstock, Conn.: Spring Publications, 1984.

Watkins, M. *Invisible Guests: The Development of Imaginal Dialogues.* Woodstock, Conn.: Spring Publications, 2000.

JOHN M. DIRKX *is professor in the higher, adult, and lifelong education unit of the Department of Educational Administration at Michigan State University.*

3

This chapter offers a conceptual map for describing different means by which expressive ways of knowing support a holistic approach to transformative learning.

Expressive Ways of Knowing and Transformative Learning

Jacqueline Davis-Manigaulte, Lyle Yorks, Elizabeth Kasl

We believe that transformative learning includes a holistic change in how a person both affectively relates to and conceptually frames his or her experience; thus, it requires a healthy interdependence between affective and rational ways of knowing. Our purpose in this chapter is to describe the role played by expressive ways of knowing in connecting affect and rationality so that transformative learning can take place.

By "expressive ways of knowing" we mean those forms of expression that engage the learner's imagination and intuition. Our analysis of imagination and intuition as intrinsic elements of holistic learning is rooted in John Heron's conceptualization of what he calls "an extended epistemology" (Heron, 1992; Yorks and Kasl, 2002). Space does not permit a full explanation of Heron's theory. Briefly, he uses the term *presentational knowing* to describe what we are calling expressive ways of knowing. According to Heron, presentational knowing happens when conceptual processes interact with imagination and intuition so as to enable learners to perceive patterns. Presentational ways of knowing include engagement with music, all the plastic arts, dance, movement, and mime, as well as all forms of myth, fable, allegory, story, and drama.

In this chapter, we offer a conceptual map for describing the different ways in which expressive ways of knowing support holistic learning. We believe that educators who work in formal education settings often use expressive activities as icebreakers or as respite from analytical thinking, but they view these activities as disconnected from what they think of as "real" learning. Our intention is to assist educators with understanding how

expressive activities are intrinsic to holistic learning so that they can be more deliberate in their practice.

We recognize that translating our map into practice requires educators to be open to their own intuitive grasp of learning situations. For this reason, we bring the ideas to life by developing an example from practice. Jaqueline Davis-Manigaulte is a university-based educator in New York City. Her story explains how she used expressive ways of knowing with young interns who were completing degrees in nutrition. The story begins with how she first drew on her own intuitive sense of why expressive activities would enhance the interns' learning.

Jackie's Story

We have a component in our organization that addresses nutrition and health issues among youth and families in targeted low-income communities, primarily through community educators. Student interns work with us, observing the community educators, teaching families and youth about nutrition, and taking on special projects as part of their degree requirements. Our faculty felt the students needed to strengthen their critical reflection skills in order to improve their understanding of the connections between field placement experiences and what they were learning in the classroom. Students were going through the motions, but they did not seem to be digging deeply into understanding the implications of what they were doing. I thought that taking on this challenge would give me a chance to put into practice what I know as an adult educator about reflection and learning from experience.

I realized that what I wanted to do with the interns was a lot like collaborative inquiry (CI), which is a systematic process of action and reflection (Bray, Lee, Smith, and Yorks, 2000; Yorks and Kasl, 2002). After two meetings with the interns, I was still wondering, How do I make the reflection come to life? When I read a book chapter by Suzanne Van Stralen (2002), I suddenly knew the answer. Suzanne had facilitated a CI with nursing managers who met in a hospital boardroom during their hectic workdays. I could visualize the group setting and could sense what it might be like to be part of her group. I could see how the nurses' situation was similar to my students' and I was excited to realize that I could use Suzanne's experience as a model for how to work with the interns.

My first two meetings with the interns had taken place in a busy space with people walking back and forth. I reserved a room for our third session that would give us privacy and set it up much like Suzanne had set up her room. By the time I came to this session, I had read and reread her chapter and had it marked up, picking out the elements that stood out for me as what I wanted to create in my session. Getting the room ready for the students, I lit candles and put on a tape of the sounds of English meadows, such as birds and rustling leaves. I was a little nervous, wondering what the

New Directions for Adult and Continuing Education • DOI: 10.1002/ace

interns would think, worrying they'd react, "Oh, boy! What is this??" However, they loved it; they just oohed and aahed about the change in environment. And they were very receptive to the activities that followed. I felt very relieved.

One of the things that stood out for me in Suzanne's work was the importance of guided visualization. So I asked the interns to close their eyes and become quiet, to feel their breath. Then I guided them to walk over a bridge into a meadow, into a pastoral setting, and to listen to the birds and smell the flowers. I asked them to breathe and feel their bodies become comfortable, to pay attention to all their senses. For the rest of the times we met, we started with a visualization to help us all come down a notch. Then we used various art activities—drawing, making collages, and using clay— to help us with reflection.

Our artwork provided a pathway for surfacing our underlying thinking. The resulting insights helped people act in new ways. One example of this was with Rachel. We did a drawing session with everyone expressing how they were feeling. Rachel drew a picture with a box in the bottom right corner closed up tight, and then she filled the rest of the page with an elliptical shape that had lots of different energy bursting. In our session, we talked about how Rachel had been reflecting for some time on how she needed to get out of the box, to think outside the box. After that session, she had a great experience of getting out of the box. She was responsible for doing some activities with youths at a health fair. The activity worked fine with the younger youths, but suddenly she was faced with a group of older youths She knew they were not going to connect with this activity, so she had to figure out what to do. She wound up drawing on another aspect of her being that had nothing to do with her bag of tricks. She had been in the army prior to coming to school, so she started saying, "I'm going to show you how to do a military drill, something like jumping jacks." They looked at her as if to say, "*Yeah, right!*" Rachel is petite and does not look like she could do anything like that. But then she did it, and she commanded them to do it, and they immediately jumped in line.

Out of this experience, Rachel realized she had this whole other reservoir of experiences. Our group talked about Rachel's realization and about how each of us is unique. Eventually the insight about each person's uniqueness led to a key learning that the interns boiled down to, "Drawing from past experience is beneficial in dealing with new challenges." By the end of the semester, the interns had identified several key learnings. I could trace each of these back to reflections that came out of their artwork.

Another important reason for using expressive ways of knowing is that it accelerates getting to know who people are. The second group I worked with had been in their internships for three weeks before I met with them. At that first meeting, I asked them to "draw something that reflects how you are feeling today in terms of your time so far with the internship."

I noticed that when we were drawing, with the meadow sounds in the background, everyone seemed to relax a little. Everyone was still very professional, but this gave us a chance to unwind a bit, and in the process, I could see they started to become more creative with colors in their drawings. By the time we got to the discussion and people elaborated on what they had drawn, everyone was open to sharing. When one person described her drawing, others would bring in a related point. For example, one woman had drawn a school of fish with one fish swimming in the opposite direction. She said, "I feel I'm in a school of fish and I'm not sure I want to swim in this direction." A number of the others agreed ("I know what you mean"). Expressive knowing helps a group get connected more quickly. It gave us a chance to learn about each other in ways that did not come out when I simply asked them, "Tell me about yourselves."

I do not think I realized until I started the process of writing this account of my experience that I have been as changed by these encounters with expressive ways of knowing as the students have been. I realized the first time I led the interns in a visualization that I had to do everything with the students. I did not want them to think that I thought I was above it all, that I did not need to learn, that I was "the teacher" telling them what to do. I told the students this was the first time I had done anything like this and we would be learning together.

I can see now that taking time out of the intense pace of work was something I benefited from greatly. "To be effective in a work environment, one must take care of oneself holistically" was another conclusion that the first group of interns put on its list of key learnings. Being with these groups was an opportunity for all of us, including me, to pause. My pause included listening or talking about what was happening with myself as well as listening and trying to help make sense out of what was happening with the interns.

How Expressive Ways of Knowing Work in Practice

Imaginal and intuitive knowing manifested in expressive forms is an important bridge between precognitive, prelinguistic experiential knowing and conceptual knowing, which is often referred to as rational or analytical knowing. Previously two of us (Yorks and Kasl, 2003) documented different pedagogical functions served by expressive forms of knowing. By examining nine case studies where expressive activities were important contributors to transformative learning (Kaltoft, 1990; Smith, 1995; Zelman, 1995; Pritchard and Sanders, 2002; Roberson, 2002; Rosenwasser, 2002; Yorks and Kasl, 2002; Paxton, 2003; Van Stralen, 2003), we analyzed learners' perceptions about these activities as contributors to learning. From interviews with adult educators whose pedagogies include various expressive activities, we collected information about pedagogical intentions as well as the educators' observations about impact on learners. Analysis of these data provided the key elements of a taxonomy for describing how expressive ways of knowing facilitate learning. We now illustrate the taxonomy's key elements by using Jackie's story, supplemented with case and interview data from the previous study.

A Taxonomy of Expressive Ways of Knowing in Practice

The pedagogical purposes for expressive practices that elicit imaginal and intuitive knowing can be divided into two general categories: (1) creating a learning environment conducive to whole-person learning and (2) working with learners within that environment.

Creating a Learning Environment Conducive to Whole-Person Learning. Expressive ways of knowing are used to create the psychological setting for transforming class meeting time into generative space within which whole-person learning can be facilitated.

Helping Learners Be Attentive to Learning. One aspect of creating this generative space is helping people make the transition from their outside worlds into a mental and emotional place that allows them to be open to learning. Often this is accomplished through adopting rituals at the beginning of the learning encounter that resonate holistically with the participants. Jackie's story provides an example. The guided visualization facilitated transition from the hectic work environment into a peaceful refuge for learning. Jackie could see how the students unwound, and as they engaged with the artistic expression, they became more creative and open to sharing. More than just markers of the beginning of a learning event, these practices, we suggest, serve to attune learners to their intentions for learning and to connect them with a sense of mutual purpose.

Creating an Empathic Field. In addition to facilitating a transition into a more holistic learning context, expressive ways of knowing provide entry to an empathic field for learning-within-relationship. The empathic field is an important dimension of the learning environment. Jackie was struck by how use of imaginal activities "accelerates getting to know who people are." Being able to know others by identifying with their experiential knowing, especially when that knowing is deeply emotional or closely tied to personal identity and values, becomes the basis for learning-within-relationship. The empathic field provides a supportive context within which difficult issues can be pursued without rupturing the relationship. For example, Penny Rosenwasser (2002) describes the opening session with Jewish women engaged in a cooperative inquiry about their internalized anti-Semitism. "At our first meeting, I encouraged the presenting of our knowledge through music, art, poetry, and story. During the meeting's reflection Geri revealed she 'felt very heard,' commenting that she had 'never had that experience on this kind of material'" (p. 54). We suggest that when Geri felt heard, she was experiencing the power of participating in an empathic field. Expressive activities enable learners to share their experiential knowing in a way that provides others with a brief portal of entry into sharing that experience and perhaps relating it to their own experiential knowing.

Working with Learners Within the Whole-Person Learning Environment. Apart from creating an environment conducive to learning, expressive pedagogical practices that engage holistic knowing directly foster the learning process in three ways.

Creating a Pathway to Felt Experience and Unconscious Knowing. Experiential knowing includes emotions, which affect people's way of being in the world. Experiential knowing is not easily communicated to either oneself or one's fellow learners. When learners work with expressive processes, they often are made aware of feelings and emotions that they are bringing to the learning encounter. When Jackie's student Rachel drew the tightly closed box and the elliptical shape bursting with energy, she made a vivid connection with her felt need to think outside the box. Subsequently, her enhanced consciousness about this desire gave her courage to discard her bag of tricks and rely on her military experience to meet an unexpected challenge. While many of us silo our experiences into separate categories, affectively they are part of the holistic reservoir of lived experience from which we draw in resolving new challenges. Through actively participating in expressive ways of knowing, learners bring the imaginal and intuitive insights contained in this reservoir of lived experience into their own awareness. With increased awareness, learners are better able to bring their affective states and conceptual sense making into alignment.

Codifying New Insight So That It Is More Accessible for Future Meaning Making. In this chapter we have described how expressive ways of knowing can bring the affective into consciousness. In addition, these ways of knowing can create an encapsulation of complex experience and ideas. If a learner creates an expressive representation of a new insight, he or she can later relive the entire learning experience by reexperiencing the expressive representation. For example, when Rachel confronted an unexpected challenge at the health fair, the simple memory of her drawing helped her reengage with her group's reflective discussion about how to think outside the box. One of the adult educators interviewed for the earlier study talked about using expressive activities to produce a bodily memory, which learners can draw on for guidance in future challenging situations. Metaphor and story are common forms of expression that carry capacities to codify. A collaborative inquiry group organized by Whitney Wherret Roberson (2002) encoded the inquiry's intention in a birthing metaphor. Encapsulating a web of complex ideas, the metaphor helped lead the group to new insights about how to facilitate transformative learning.

Creating a Lived Experience of What the Learner Seeks to Understand. Often educators may want to evoke the experience that learners are trying to learn more about. For example, Elizabeth Kasl reports being part of a synergic inquiry in which a group of white people had been talking about and trying to conceptualize their experience of separation and alienation. When they used movement and symbols to communicate their experience to a group of African Americans, they evoked in themselves a felt experience of alienation. The next time they came together, their conceptual reflection about alienation drew on their shared experience and was more insightful than it had been previously. In addition, the African Americans who watched the presentation reported feeling empathically toward the white group's alienation (Yorks and Kasl, 2002).

The Educator as Holistic Learner

There is another aspect evident in Jackie's story that is typical of the educators we studied. Jackie has come to realize that she has "been as changed by the encounters with expressive ways of knowing as the students have been." Her realization is consistent with other educators' perceptions about the importance of developing themselves as whole-person learners. Educators interviewed for the previous study spoke about the importance of being fully present in their relationships with learners and about being fully grounded in their own multiple ways of knowing.

This connection between the educator's inner life and engaging learners as whole persons is part of the explanation for Jackie's willingness to take a risk and engage in a practice that was foreign, overcoming her uncertainty about bringing this kind of activity into her university workplace. "In a sense, I have been falling back on a natural part of my experience that I have never brought to the office or to my work. I do these kinds of things in my own life, but I was afraid to bring my whole self to work. What has changed for me is really trusting who I am and allowing myself to be. It's richer and I have more to share, by being more of me, not feeling any longer that I have to compartmentalize everything." Suzanne's chapter had an impact on Jackie because it resonated with her own holistic knowing. If educators are going to be effective in helping learners develop and transform through holistic learning, they have to be willing to engage themselves holistically as well. This goes to the heart of the idea of the educator as colearner.

Conclusion

We have described strategies through which adult educators can effectively tap into imagination and intuition by using expressive ways of knowing. Transformative learning involves a person's experiencing profound changes in how the learner understands and relates to some significant aspect of his or her world. The practices described in this chapter are powerful ways of both creating the learning space and facilitating the learning process necessary for transformative learning.

Of course, in any situation, how the educator combines these practices requires making informed judgments regarding the learners involved and explaining the educator's rationale. Fostering transformative learning requires taking learners out of their comfort zone, both cognitively and affectively, while providing sufficient support. Using expressive ways of knowing can also take the educator out of his or her comfort zone. Jackie notes, for example, that despite her intuitive feeling that what she intended to do was right, "I was a little concerned about bringing expressive ways of knowing into my workplace. I have one colleague who would see me preparing for the group and jokingly remark, 'Oh there she goes again. She's got the candles and the clay!!' When I started the project I thought I needed to explain what I was doing to our director. I wanted her to learn about the project from me rather than from anyone else. So I went to her and explained that I was using an approach to adult learning that I was studying in my doctoral program. I made sure she knew my professor had written articles about the process I was trying. She thought what I was doing was great. That was all I needed to hear! . . . Eventually I did presentations locally and at our state conference based on my collaborative inquiry experiences."

Finally, the adventure of working with these methods transforms the educator as well. We close with Jackie as she reflects on the experience of bringing her whole self to work: "I had been out meeting with some program officers regarding a potential funding opportunity and was excited about what had happened. When I came back to the office, I was sharing some of my thoughts with my director about what I thought we needed to do to move forward with the project. At the end of the conversation, we came to the same conclusion about something at the same time and I, without thinking first, just gave him a high five. Giving your boss a high five because you feel comfortable enough that you can be yourself. That is far from normal protocol."

References

Bray, J., Lee, J., Smith, L., and Yorks, L. *Collaborative Inquiry in Practice: Action, Reflection, and Making Meaning.* Thousand Oaks, Calif.: Sage, 2000.

Heron, J. *Feeling and Personhood: Psychology in Another Key.* Thousand Oaks, Calif.: Sage, 1992.

Kaltoft, G. "Music and Emancipatory Learning in Three Community Education Programs." Unpublished doctoral dissertation, Teachers College, Columbia University, 1990.

Paxton, D. E. "Facilitating Transformation of White Consciousness Among European-American People: A Case Study of a Cooperative Inquiry." Unpublished doctoral dissertation, California Institute of Integral Studies, 2003.

Pritchard, C., and Sanders, P. "Weaving Our Stories as They Weave Us." In L. Yorks and E. Kasl (eds.), *Collaborative Inquiry as a Strategy for Adult Learning: Creating Space for Generative Learning.* New Directions in Adult and Continuing Education, no. 94. San Francisco: Jossey-Bass, 2002.

Roberson, W. W. "Midwife to a Learning Community: Spirit as Co-Inquirer." In L. Yorks and E. Kasl (eds.), *Collaborative Inquiry as a Strategy for Adult Learning: Creating Space for Generative Learning.* New Directions in Adult and Continuing Education, no. 94. San Francisco: Jossey-Bass, 2002.

Rosenwasser, P. "Exploring Internalized Oppression and Healing Strategies." In L. Yorks and E. Kasl (eds.), *Collaborative Inquiry as a Strategy for Adult Learning: Creating Space for Generative Learning*. New Directions for Adult and Continuing Education, no. 94. San Francisco: Jossey-Bass, 2002.

Smith, L. L. "Collaborative Inquiry as an Adult Learning Strategy." *Dissertation Abstracts International,* 1995, *56*(7), 2533. (University Microfilms No. AAC95–39867)

Van Stralen, S. "Making Sense of One's Experience in the Workplace." In L. Yorks and E. Kasl (eds.), *Collaborative Inquiry as a Strategy for Adult Learning: Creating Space for Generative Learning.* New Directions for Adult and Continuing Education, no. 94. San Francisco: Jossey-Bass, 2002.

Van Stralen, S. "Renewal and Human Flourishing—The Development of Epistemological Capacities Through Transformative Learning and Multiple Ways of Knowing: A Case Study." Unpublished doctoral dissertation, California Institute of Integral Studies, 2003.

Yorks, L., & Kasl, E. "Toward a Theory and Practice for Whole-Person Learning: Reconceptualizing Experience and the Role of Affect." *Adult Education Quarterly,* 2002, *52,* 176–192.

Yorks, L., & Kasl, E. "Through the Looking Glass: A Taxonomy for Presentational Knowing." In *Proceedings for the Forty-Second Annual Adult Education Research Conference.* San Francisco: San Francisco State University, 2003.

Zelman, A. W. "Answering the Question: How Is Learning Experienced through Collaborative Inquiry?" *Dissertation Abstracts International,* 1995, *56*(7), 2534. (University Microfilms No. AAC9S-39885)

JACQUELINE DAVIS-MANIGAULTE is a doctoral candidate at Teachers College, Columbia University.

LYLE YORKS is associate professor of adult education at Teachers College, Columbia University, where he is director of the Adult Education Guided Intensive Study doctoral program.

ELIZABETH KASL is adjunct faculty at the California Institute of Integral Studies in San Francisco, where she was formerly professor of transformative learning.

4

This chapter discusses the challenges of fostering spirituality in the higher education classroom and its relationship to the practice of transformative learning.

Engaging Spirituality in the Transformative Higher Education Classroom

Derise E. Tolliver, Elizabeth J. Tisdell

Rebecca e-mails her instructor the morning after class to say that she could not sleep after the evening's discussion about purpose in adult education. She describes a strongly felt need to incorporate a less individualistic focus in her academic program. Frank begins a morning meditation ritual after taking a course where the instructor includes a guided visualization during each class session. He says that it helps with his ability to concentrate and express his creativity. In her evaluation of a course that integrates multiple ways of knowing as part of its curriculum, a student writes, "Anxiety is reduced when things are put in a proper perspective. Spiritual touch keeps us in touch. This class provided a vehicle to see myself so differently from my daily routines and to know myself a little more." The comments from these students reflect what is increasingly being discussed in the discourses of many fields, including adult education: the presence of spirituality in the higher education classroom and the importance of its recognition and engagement in transformative learning.

To make our definition of transformative learning explicit, we believe that transformative learning creates a more expansive understanding of the world regarding how one sees and experiences both others and one's self and is grounded in one's entire being. Such learning increases one's sense of an ability to make a difference in the world and leads to a greater sense of purpose and meaning. In the broad sense, this indeed corresponds to much of what Mezirow and Associates (2000) have discussed in their book; how-

NEW DIRECTIONS FOR ADULT AND CONTINUING EDUCATION, no. 109, Spring 2006 © 2006 Wiley Periodicals, Inc.
Published online in Wiley InterScience (www.interscience.wiley.com) • DOI: 10.1002/ace.206

ever, none of the authors of that book explicitly discusses the role of spirituality in transformative learning, which is our intent here.

We believe that learning is more likely to be transformative if it permeates one's whole self, which has a spiritual component, rather than being confined to the rational realm of critically reflecting on assumptions. Transformative learning is best facilitated through engaging multiple dimensions of being, including the rational, affective, spiritual, imaginative, somatic, and sociocultural domains through relevant content and experiences. While higher education has traditionally confined itself largely to the rational dimension, we believe that it is possible to engage multiple aspects of being in the adult higher education classroom, including the spiritual dimension to facilitate transformative learning. Thus, our intent in this chapter is three-fold: (1) to define what we mean by spirituality, (2) to explain why we believe it is relevant in the higher education classroom in attempts at transformative education, and (3) to discuss how we foster it in practice. We will consider some of the possibilities and limitations of drawing on spirituality and transformative learning in the higher education classroom.

What Is Spirituality?

Spirituality is a somewhat elusive concept, but the many authors in higher education who discuss it at least implicitly attempt to define what it is (Astin, 2004; hooks, 2003, English and Gillen, 2000; Palmer, 2000; Wuthnow, 2001). As we have noted elsewhere (Tisdell, 2003; Tisdell and Tolliver, 2003), what is common in these discussions is that spirituality is about a connection to what is referred to by various names, such as the Life Force, God, a higher power or purpose, Great Spirit, or Buddha Nature. It is about meaning making and a sense of wholeness, healing, and the interconnectedness of all things. Spirituality is different from religion: it is about an individual's journey toward wholeness, whereas religions are organized communities of faith that often provide meaningful community rituals that serve as a gateway to the sacred. But because there is a spiritual dimension to all religions, spirituality and religion are interrelated for many people, particularly if their conscious manifestation of spirituality takes place primarily in the context of an organized religion.

Spirituality also is about developing a more authentic identity. As many authors have noted, those who value spirituality believe that there is a divine spark in each person that is central to his or her core essence or authentic self. Those who value spirituality generally believe that it is possible for learners to come to a greater understanding of their core essence through transformative learning experiences that help them reclaim their authenticity. Cranton (Chapter One, this volume) has discussed the notion of authenticity in detail in relation to transformative learning. Our point here is that this notion of moving toward authenticity is also core to what spirituality is about, though we are always in the process of this motion.

Another important dimension to spirituality often ignored by authors is its connection to culture. Faith development theorist James Fowler (1981) suggests that spirituality is partly related to how people construct knowledge through "symbolic processes" and "unconscious structuring processes" (p. 103) manifested through image, symbol, and music. But these aspects of spirituality are always manifested culturally. It is because spirituality connects these "unconscious and symbolic processes" through image, symbol, metaphor, poetry, art, and music that it is easy to draw on spirituality in the classroom without pushing an explicitly spiritual agenda. Many authors and researchers have noted that in its connection to the expression of "unconscious and symbolic processes," spirituality often connects to creativity through imagination and creative expression (Parks, 2000; Wuthnow, 2001). Furthermore, as such expressions are shared with others, spirituality often leads to and helps create community (hooks, 2003; Palmer, 1998).

Why Spirituality in the Adult Higher Education Classroom?

Given that higher education has traditionally been about the role of rationality in learning, one might wonder how spirituality could possibly be relevant in the higher education classroom. Higher education is about the construction and dissemination of knowledge, and human beings construct knowledge through multiple means. But an exploration and analysis of the world of ideas need not be limited to considerations of only rational modes of thought. As neurologist and author Antonio Damasio (1999) notes, rational ideas are better understood and learned if they are anchored in one's entire be rather than as facts stored in one's short-term memory to be spit back on a test, only to be forgotten afterward. Engaging learning in multiple dimensions, including the rational, affective, somatic, spiritual, and sociocultural, will increase the chances that new knowledge is actually constructed and embodied, thus having the potential to be transformative.

Many adults identify spirituality as a major organizing principle that gives their lives meaning and informs their life choices. But if, as Mezirow and Associates (2000) note, transformative learning is partly about the transformation of meaning schemes and spirituality is partly about meaning making, often the transformation of meaning schemes naturally connects to the spiritual and can lead to transformation on either the individual or sociocultural level. Boyd and Myers (1988), for example, view transformative learning as an intuitive, creative, emotional process, while Tobin Hart (2000) discusses evolutionary consciousness as being grounded in spirituality. Educator Parker Palmer (1998) refers to graced moments in teaching and learning in the higher education classroom and gives examples where some larger truth was told, the classroom was experienced as a learning community, and members were invited into their greater authenticity.

Talking more specifically about social transformation, David Abalos (1998) discusses the importance of reclaiming four faces (the personal, political, historical, and sacred) of one's being as part of the transformation process for culturally marginalized communities. The sacred face is related to spirituality that is grounded in their own cultural community, by claiming and reclaiming images, symbols, ways of being, and celebrating that are sacred to individuals and the community as a whole. Abalos suggests that as human beings free their sacred face, they often take action to change the status quo. Sharing one's stories of engaging with these four faces in light of readings and other course experiences in the classroom community helps people see from multiple perspectives. Hearing others' stories and ideas in new ways also facilitates greater creativity, and as Maxine Greene (1997) suggests, engaging imagination and creativity that helps people develop a broadened perspective is what higher education is about. Yet as Wuthnow (2001) notes, this engagement with creativity often touches on the spiritual as well.

What Does Spirituality Look Like in Practice?

There are numerous ways to engage the spiritual dimension in the higher education classroom that have the potential to facilitate transformative learning without imposing a religious or spiritual agenda. It is important to emphasize here that educational practice informed by spirituality does not mean proselytizing lectures or the imposition of a dogmatic agenda, or even necessarily discussing spirituality directly. Rather, it involves authenticity, openness, acceptance, and honoring of the various dimensions of how people learn and construct knowledge by incorporating activities that include attention to the affective, somatic, imaginative, symbolic, cultural, and communal, as well as the rational. Such multiple engagements are often experienced as both spiritual and transformative. We can indeed draw on our own spirituality without directly discussing it, as Helminiak (2001) suggests, without being imperialist. Elsewhere (Tisdell, 2003; Tisdell and Tolliver, 2003) we have offered a model of a spiritually grounded and culturally responsive pedagogy for transformative learning that can be applied to practice. It includes the following components:

- An emphasis on authenticity of teachers and students
- An environment that fosters the exploration of multiple forms of knowledge production including:
  The cognitive (through readings and discussion of ideas)
  The affective and relational (through connection with other people and of ideas to life experience)
  The symbolic, spiritual, and imaginative domain (through drawing on symbol and metaphor in the use of art form such as poetry, art, music, drama, and ritual)
  Readings that reflect the cultures of the members of the class and the larger community

New Directions for Adult and Continuing Education • DOI: 10.1002/ace

Exploration of individual and communal dimensions of cultural and other dimensions of identity
Collaborative work that envisions and presents manifestations of multiple dimensions of learning and strategies for change
- Celebration of learning and provision for closure to the course
- Recognition of the limitations of the higher education classroom and that transformation is an ongoing process that takes time

Creating an environment that invites multiple dimensions of learning includes attending to the cognitive, the affective, the relational, the imaginal, and the symbolic dimensions of learning. Courses in higher education always need to include readings that deal with ideas and theoretical issues relevant to the course content, but the affective and connective dimensions can be incorporated in papers and class discussions as well. One can engage the symbolic domain or the cultural imagination as well as these other domains of learning that some might map to as spiritual. These also could be experienced as transformative.

An important element is setting up an environment that both invites people into their greater authenticity and draws on multiple forms of knowledge construction right from the beginning. We are women of different racial and cultural backgrounds and teach in different kinds of higher education institutions, and each of us accomplishes this in somewhat different ways. We present here how we do this in our separate and unique voices.

Derise Tolliver. I am a clinical psychologist by training, teaching adults in a higher education setting. My professional identity is grounded in my African and African American cultural identity, deeply rooted in spirituality with a commitment to balance, harmony, understanding, and social justice. I believe that when we "remember" who we are as individuals and in collaboration with others, as well as "re-member" fragmented aspects of ourselves that are often devalued, disregarded, or dismissed, we can be more successful in our academic, professional, personal, and collective endeavors. My intention is to assist learners in their remembering and re-membering. This can lead to transformative learning.

In writing about how this is fostered in my practice, I, like many of my students when approaching their academic work, faced a blank screen and many blocks to expression. Once I gave myself permission to tap into something other than my academic voice, I found that I was able to write more easily and fluidly (and, I hope, in a more engaging manner). What follows, expressed as a poem, is a description of how one of my classes might be holistically experienced by a learner:

Coming from a hectic day,
Entering into an ordinary classroom
    bigger than its four walls would reveal.
Glowing candle

warms the way to connect
with what is already known.
Deep wisdom waiting to be retrieved from mind, spirit, body
    course content important, but how is it relevant to me, my life, my
world?
    course content, a house for the spiritual.
Calming breath,
    connecting to the present,
    presence,
    awareness coming.
Centering on breath,
Centering on sensation of being
    now, present, in this space and time.
Breathing in, intentionally—my knowing, strength and peace.
Breathing out, intentionally—ignorance, tension, that which is not peace.
Sitting in a circle,
    no hiding behind someone else,
    risky, yet opening
    connected on both sides and through the middle.
Empty chair in middle of the room
    reminding of connections to others
    and although they are not physically present
    their ideas, words, energy are.
Someone sings their own song.
    Another says, "hearing Aretha takes me to another place,
    makes me whole."
    Someone else, different culture, different words,
    sings the same feeling.
    She who learns, teaches—
    proverbs help guide us.
    "You must eat the elephant one bite at a time"—
    reassuring that my rhythm is fine,
    at least in this space.
    Rhythm, movement.
    We dance together.
    We create, individually and together.
    We think,
    feel,
    act,
    compose, and
    draw.
    We make meaning.
    We hear words,
    words sometimes not heard in other classes:
    purpose

heart
compassion
soul
love
spirit.
Can I celebrate? name my passion?
I am celebrated for being . . . me.
We are celebrated for being . . . we,
   in this sacred space of learning.

The affirmation of my poetic voice and the validation of its place and role in my professional work transformed the experience of writing into a more authentic, meaningful, and enjoyable act. Similarly, the incorporation of contemplative practices and the spiritual, plus the insights that can emerge from multiple ways of knowing and expression, can support transformative learning in adult education.

Libby Tisdell. I am an educator—a white, middle-class woman teaching doctoral students in adult education. How I attempt to engage learning that will more likely be grounded in participants' entire being is that in addition to the usual syllabus and books that are a part of the opening class, I also try to set up an environment where students will explore the meaning that they map to symbol. There is typically a heavy reading load in my classes, and content is explored from many cultural perspectives. But in addition to the obvious academic readings and scholarly writing that is part of doctoral course work, I bring symbols of the elements of the world—earth, wind, fire, and water, as well as other symbols of culture and knowing—because learning takes place in the context of our life experience in the world, and these symbols can serve as a reminder of that.

For some people, this sense of symbol can implicitly take learning to what the heart of spirituality is about: the interconnectedness of all things and a sense of knowing through imagination that some connect with creativity and spirituality, though I rarely use the term *spirituality* in my classes. I also begin each class with a brief check-in of joys and difficulties that have been a part of the students' learning lives since the last time we met, which brings a sense of affect, emotion, and groundedness in real-life experience. This five-minute activity is an attempt to create a learning community that honors the life experiences of the learners and sets the stage for the use of other modes of learning in addition to the rational.

Throughout the course, students engage in at least one long-term assignment that is collaborative and do at least one collaborative teaching presentation where they engage multiple modes of knowledge construction with the class, in addition to writing the typical academic paper about the readings and their learning. The closing session always includes a celebration of learning, which may involve music, dance, or other ways of engaging our bodies, minds, and spirits. It taps into and expresses that which is

New Directions for Adult and Continuing Education • DOI: 10.1002/ace

often beyond words that students often connect to as part of their deeper and more authentic self. It is this becoming more conscious in creative ways, integrated with rationality and affect, that offers a sense of creative imagination and hope that learners bring with them as well as the academic content knowledge. This integrated sense of knowledge is what is often transformational, and for some it is spiritual as well.

Hinting at Ritual

It is clear that when we engage multiple forms of knowledge, there are particular components that might be useful to think about in relation to transformative learning. The use of symbol and image, the arts, attention to affect, and rationality needs no further explanation. But there is also a hint of ritual in what we do, in the sense that there is some regular form to the shape of the learning environment. Admittedly, rituals are already established in most classrooms; however, in our practices, these rituals are intentionally more inclusive of the spiritual and appreciative of various cultural expression.

Ritual is deeply connected to our human nature and an important aspect of the learning environment (Some, 1998; Zhang, 2004). Durkheim defined ritual as "the mechanism that produces ideas charged with social significance" (Collins, 1994, p. 212). Conventionally described as repetitive and compulsive behavior, these standard conceptions miss the sacred quality of ritual, the unplanned aspect that makes spiritual knowing into forms of expression that can be experienced and shared in the context of community (Teish, 2004). Although ritual is not orchestrated, there is a certain process associated with it (Some, 1998). It can provide a holistic experience of learning, especially when there is an "immediate acting out that bridges and unifies the somatic and ideational, the bodily and the mythical" (Doty, as cited in Hill, 2004, p. 6). Many of these aspects of ritual are present in our classes, particularly in the gathering and closing to the class, but also in how the learning activities and discussions are typically structured. These rituals can be diverse, fluid, evolving, and multicultural, as well as individualistic, and can provide collective opportunities of making meaning (Hill, 2004; Zhang, 2004). In the transformative learning classroom, the intention is that the sense of ritual we develop at the beginning of class will serve to challenge exclusionary practices and hegemonic structures through the functions of communication, significance, sanctuary, and connection. Some (1998) has stated that transformation and healing cannot occur without ritual.

Rhythm activities, such as music, sound, dance, and movement, are often used to engage kinesthetic ways of knowing and expressing meaning in the world. These elements also may function to help learners access other forms of information that are not necessarily at the level of conscious awareness. They often allow us to connect with the aesthetic energies that facilitate learning. Arranging the classroom in a way that promotes engagement reflects the active use of space. Designating certain areas of the classroom

New Directions for Adult and Continuing Education • DOI: 10.1002/ace

or using areas outside the formal classroom that represent particular aspects of learning also constitutes the engagement of space. Finally, objects such as symbols or the use of poetry, proverb, or metaphor take on particular meaning because they can represent something significant in the transformative learning environment. They might be cues, or reflect aspects of the self, that connect specifically to the course content.

Caveats, Possibilities, and Conclusions

Because of the often evocative nature of the subject of spirituality, integration of this concept in educational practice may be distinctively challenging. Fenwick (2001) wisely cautions educators to be critically reflective of our efforts to ensure that our motivation and use of spiritual pedagogies enhance, facilitate, and support the growth and wholeness of learners. At the same time, we concur with hooks (2003), who encourages our willingness to transgress against mainstream cultural taboos that silence the passion for addressing issues of soul and spirit.

Indeed, we must be careful in how we incorporate activities and ways of knowing that some might view as spiritual. As educators, we must always be aware of the power differentials between ourselves and the learners in our classrooms. When our practice is informed by our authenticity and fullness of being that includes the spiritual, even if the word is never mentioned, we invite learners to participate in the learning process at their own level of desire and comfort, without expectations that they will share our perspectives and passions. Our concern is not so much the cultivation of a particular type of spiritual awareness. Rather, we are committed to learning that makes a difference in learners' lives and increases their sense of knowing the content of the course in their heads, their hearts, their souls, and their entire being—that has meaning to them and makes a difference in the world.

Spirituality can involve not only positive and constructive understandings, but also struggle and confrontation of the more shadowy aspects of human existence (Bennett, 2003; Fenwick, 2001). Making it visible in the classroom may be uncomfortable, and many adult educators may feel unprepared for this challenge. It is risky, in part, because as we attend to the spiritual, we are also required to engage authentically as people, not only as instructors and students. Furthermore, spirit is powerful. However, the most powerful moments we have had in classes are when participants take risks and share their authentic selves and their connection to others through their own honesty and creativity as they relate course content to their lives. Perhaps it feels risky because it feels as though we also cannot control what feels so powerful.

In conclusion, spirituality is a deep phenomenon; its presence and value are independent of specific course content, and its connection to the development and growth of the learner is present in the learning process itself. We can embrace and embody spirituality in our actions and approach to work without ever explicitly using the word *spirituality*. Since it is always present in the learning environment, it is unnecessary to pursue it directly. However, numerous classroom activities, exercises, and means are available that can support and facilitate the expression of what is already present. Manifestations of spirituality often happen spontaneously—in dramatic presentations on a theme in the reading, in visual representation of the meaning of a concept, in creation of poetry in response to an exercise, and in the call for stillness following an evocative experience. It is present whenever people's authenticity becomes visible in new ways and more connected to others. It is this openness to our deepest selves, other people, other perspectives, and possibilities that deeply fuels the transformation process. If this is a part of what spirituality is about as well, clearly it has a place in transformative learning.

References

Abalos, D. *La Communidad Latina in the United States.* Westport, Conn.: Praeger, 1998.

Astin, A. "Why Spirituality Deserves a Central Place in Liberal Education." *Liberal Education,* 2004, *90*(2), 34–41.

Bennett, J. *Academic Life: Hospitality, Ethics, and Spirituality.* Bolton, Mass.: Anker Publishing, 2003.

Boyd, R. D., and Myers, J. G. "Transformative Education." *International Journal of Lifelong Education,* 1988, *7*(4), 261–284.

Collins, R. *Four Sociological Traditions.* New York: Oxford University Press, 1994.

Damasio, A. *The Feeling of What Happens.* New York: Harcourt, 1999.

English, L. M., and Gillen, M. A. "Addressing the Spiritual Dimensions of Adult Learning." In L. M. English and M. A. Gillen (eds.), *Addressing the Spiritual Dimensions of Adult Learning: What Educators Can Do.* New Directions for Adult and Continuing Education, no 85. San Francisco: Jossey-Bass, 2000.

Fenwick, T. "Critical Questions for Pedagogical Engagement of Spirituality." *Adult Learning,* 2001, *12*(3), 10–12.

Fowler, J. *Stages of Faith: The Psychology of Human Development and the Quest for Meaning.* San Francisco: HarperSanFrancisco, 1981.

Greene, M. "Metaphor and Multiples: Representation, the Arts, and History." *Phi Delta Kappan,* 1997, *78*(5), 387–395.

Hart, T. *From Information to Transformation: Education for the Evolution of Consciousness.* New York: Peter Lang, 2000.

Helminiak, D. A. "Treating Spiritual Issues in Secular Psychotherapy." *Counseling and Values,* 2001, *45*(3), 163–190.

Hill, P. "African Presence in the Americas: Rituals and Rites of Passage." Retrieved Nov. 1, 2004, from www.ritesofpassage.org/bookchapter.doc.

hooks, b. *Teaching Community.* New York: Routledge, 2003.

Mezirow, J., and Associates (eds.). *Learning as Transformation: Critical Perspectives on a Theory in Progress.* San Francisco: Jossey-Bass, 2000.

Palmer, P. *The Courage to Teach.* San Francisco: Jossey-Bass, 1998.

Palmer, P. *Let Your Life Speak.* San Francisco: Jossey-Bass, 2000.

Parks, S. D. *Big Questions, Worthy Dreams.* San Francisco: Jossey-Bass, 2000.

Some, M. *The Healing Wisdom of Africa.* New York: Putnam, 1998.

Teish, L. "Art as Meditation Syllabus." Retrieved November 8, 2004, from http://www.creationspirituality.net/syl%20750.htm.

Tisdell, E. *Exploring Spirituality and Culture in Adult and Higher Education.* San Francisco: Jossey-Bass, 2003.

Tisdell, E., and Tolliver, E. "Claiming a Sacred Face: The Role of Spirituality and Cultural identity in Transformative Adult Higher Education." *Journal of Transformative Education,* 2003, *1*(4), 368–392.

Wuthnow, R. *Creative Spirituality: The Way of the Artist.* Berkeley: University of California Press, 2001.

Zhang, M. "The Online Instructor and Rituals of Learning: A Durkheimian Approach to Online Education." 1999. Retrieved Nov. 8, 2004, from http://www.people.vcu.edu/~mzhang/final.htm.

DERISE E. TOLLIVER *is associate professor at DePaul University, Chicago.*

ELIZABETH J. TISDELL *is associate professor at Penn State University Harrisburg, Middletown, Pennsylvania.*

5

This chapter uses the classroom experiences of two black women professors as a lens to examine how transformational theory affects learning and teaching. It also explores the ways in which dimensions of power have an impact on student-teacher interactions.

Transformational Teaching and the Practices of Black Women Adult Educators

Juanita Johnson-Bailey, Mary V. Alfred

Recently a colleague asked me, "Juanita, why are there no black women scholars in adult education writing about transformational learning?" Dumbfounded, I could not answer his question. He continued, "From my perspective, many of the black women in adult education seem to be about transformative learning and teaching in their scholarship and in their classrooms." Still at a loss for words, I had to agree with his observation. This chapter is an answer to his charge, and together with another black woman adult educator, we share our perspectives on transformational learning and teaching for transformation.

Juanita's Journey

As a young "colored" child growing up in the segregated South in the 1950s, transformational learning saved my life. As I matured into a precocious "Negro" adolescent, an outspoken race-conscious young black adult, and most currently as a black feminist scholar, transformational learning kept me sane and sustained me. Yet my transformational learning is not the learning set forth by Mezirow (1975, 1997) and Freire (1970). Rather, it is a learning that is bound by my cultural roots and one that can be identified through the writings of the Harlem Renaissance scholars and in the slave narratives. The transformational learning theory of the adult education literature introduced by Mezirow and Freire speaks to how adults use learn-

NEW DIRECTIONS FOR ADULT AND CONTINUING EDUCATION, no. 109, Spring 2006 © 2006 Wiley Periodicals, Inc.
Published online in Wiley InterScience (www.interscience.wiley.com) • DOI: 10.1002/ace.207

ing to make meaning of major life events and changes. This adult learning theory primarily addresses the individual's capacity to use critical reflection and other rational processes to engage in meaning making. Focusing on the individual's mental processes, the theory has been critiqued as not significantly addressing the relationship between the individual, communities, and society at large. This way of examining meaning making largely ignores culturally bound group learning experiences. My primary transformative learning experiences are culturally bound and are not individualistic or confined to my adult years.

My first experience with transformational learning, as I remember, occurred when I was five years old. My mother and a neighbor told me that I could no longer play with my best friend, Dianne. They explained that we had come to that age where, although she would continue to come home with Mrs. Threat, her family's maid and our neighbor, Dianne could not come over to play with me. School-age children of different races were not allowed to play together.

This lesson on race, on difference, on power, would become more sophisticated and theoretical over my life span, but it was, alas, the first of many such lessons that would transform my way of thinking, my way of moving freely through American society, and ultimately my way of existing. This first critical lesson on race began to hone my analysis of race in Western society. However, the lesson did not embitter me or turn me against any one group. I did not blame Dianne, her mother, my mother, or Mrs. Threat. I understood at this early age that there was a system at work. To this day, I still think of Dianne; I wonder what happened to her and miss her. There have been many Diannes in my life over the years, and still systems of power rear their heads to continue this lesson on transformative learning.

My classroom teaching, where I seek to lay the groundwork for transformational learning, has grown out of my background as a military brat, as a black student growing up in the segregated and desegregated southern United States, and as a nontraditional adult learner in a higher education setting. I have been in positions of enfranchisement and disenfranchisement, privilege and underprivilege, and I have found that each one of these positions has shaped the way that I function in the classroom.

I do not think I am unique among black women my age. In our early years, we were taught and had to learn difficult lessons that would change our ways of existing in this world and would ultimately keep us safe. Understanding the concept of power and how its corresponding social locations operate within societal hierarchies is a lesson that most disenfranchised group members understand and operationalize throughout their lives. This knowledge is necessary when a person is not a member of the norm group and exists in a zone of constant negotiation because of the invisible knapsack of racial baggage (Johnson-Bailey and Cervero, 2000).

As a black woman, I am cognizant that transformational learning is about change and that the ability to promote and engender change is connected to an interplay of power between the student and the teacher: How does the student gauge his or her position? How does the student perceive the teacher's position? What does the student have to gain or lose by changing? And how will the student's interests be affected by changing? Maybe it is an intimate awareness of how power and social position figure into transformational learning, which black women educators carry with them, that prevents them from seeing transformational learning as something outside ourselves. Most of my black women colleagues see transformational learning as the only medium in which we exist, learn, and teach. Since it is the air we breathe, maybe we just take it for granted and do not attend to or claim it sufficiently.

But rather than speak for all black women in adult education, I appealed to my circle of black women colleagues, which includes four black women scholars who represent a collective sixty-five years in the adult education field. Each agreed that there was an intentional transformational component to their teaching, but as scholars, none of us used the theoretical concept of transformational teaching in the many articles that we have collectively written about teaching and learning. Over the next few weeks, I began a dialogue with one of my circle colleagues, Mary Alfred. Although we grew up worlds apart, our stories of how and why we came to transformational teaching are similar.

Mary's Journey

When I made the decision in 1975 to migrate from the Caribbean to the United States to join my husband, who was then in the military, I did not fathom the magnitude of the changes that I would have to endure. At the time, the word *transformation* was not in my vocabulary. Before migrating, I had completed teacher's college and was an elementary school principal at the tender age of twenty-one. I was a visible community activist and change agent, viewed by my people as an emerging leader. I enjoyed a high degree of social capital and saw few boundaries to my personal and professional development. I lived in a world where black people were lords and masters of their universe and where students who showed academic promise were nurtured by the family, the school, and the community, thus contributing to their development into successful adults.

Upon my arrival in the United States, that world collapsed. I arrived to find a country racially divided, where blacks were relegated to second-class citizenship and where one's worth as a human being was defined by the color of her skin and by her power to amass material wealth. As a young black woman who had no material wealth, the place prescribed for me was a space at the margins, where I was expected to remain invisible and unobtrusive. The dilemma for me resulted from my attempts to make meaning of the world I had entered within the context of the world I had left behind. I was searching in my new geographical space for the cultural values, expec-

New Directions for Adult and Continuing Education • DOI: 10.1002/ace

tations, and social capital resources that shaped my worldview on my island of Saint Lucia. This search for meaning in the midst of internal turmoil is what I would later come to know as transformational learning (Mezirow, 1990, 2000).

As a result of my experiences with border crossing, with coming to terms with what it means to be a minority in a majority white culture, with ongoing discrimination and the silent internalization of the oppression, and finally liberating myself from the oppression through knowledge and dialogue with self and others, my practice today comes from the soul. Because of the many experiences through which I have lived and my understanding of them as they shape my worldview, I use my spiritual self to guide my practice as an adult educator who aims to transform ideology and practice. I claim not to have the power to transform people but to provide opportunities for people to understand their frames of reference and use that knowledge for their own transformation.

Different Journeys, Same Destination

And so we have traveled different paths to arrive at transformational learning, and, accordingly, we have different perspectives on transformational learning. Yet our positions on the margins as women who share a common black ancestry guide our teaching with its resulting philosophy that revolves around three key concepts: inclusion, empowerment, and intellectual growth. By emphasizing inclusion, we are affirming that we want all students to participate in our classes and that we know for some groups who are characteristically silent or silenced this may involve a conscious effort on our part to make space for that student's voice. Directly connected to the issue of inclusion is the concept of empowerment, which does not connote for us the process of self-actualization often discussed in the literature but instead means that the student has a sense of belongingness and equity as a full member of the class collective. Again, working toward an environment where the student is empowered involves managing classroom dynamics to ensure that student-student, teacher-student, and curriculum-class exchanges are positive and constructive. It is our goal to try to ensure that students experience our classrooms as safe spaces where they can openly express their doubts, confront the unknown, and carve out and claim their own intellectual space. We believe in constructing a participatory educational environment that is grounded in respect.

Finally, it is important to always remember that an ideal teaching environment is built on reciprocity. Our students bring a wealth of experience and knowledge from their varying histories, contexts, geographies, and biographies. It is our responsibility to recognize, highlight, and honor their contributions. Therefore, we must always act as a conduit in helping them toward self-expression and in developing critical thinking skills. Challenging students to think critically and opening ourselves up to be challenged

New Directions for Adult and Continuing Education • DOI: 10.1002/ace

in return contributes to their intellectual growth, to our intellectual growth, and to improving and invigorating the classroom setting.

Another aspect of reciprocity involves the willingness of black women educators to engage in personal critical reflection with the students and evoke the interdependency that makes the process of transformational learning and teaching transparent and synergistic. Our dream for our students is that they use what they learn in our classrooms to become active, informed, and responsible world citizens.

It is a dream that did not begin with us and is not confined to our adult education frameworks. The teachers of Mary's homogeneous Saint Lucia and the teachers of Juanita's segregated southern schooling shared similar dreams that crossed cultural boundaries, and both sets of teachers nurtured a passion for social justice and the valuing of all voices. In critiquing the academic stance of black women as students and educators, Mirza (2004) writes:

> Black women, who have been, after all, theorized in our dominant academic discourse as "the most oppressed," deemed the least "visible," and the least empowered, the most marginal of groups, do relatively well. They appear to strive for inclusivity. However, no one wants to look at their success, their desire for inclusivity. They are out of place, disrupting and untidy. They do not fit. The notion of their agency and difference is problematic for the limited essentialist and mechanical social reproduction theories that dominate our explanations of black female inequality. . . . Black female agency has remained invisible in the masculinist discourse of "race" and social change [pp. 201–203].

A great tradition of black women as emancipatory educators exists in the annals of adult educators: Septima Clarke and Highlander; the countless and unnamed black women who poured south during Reconstruction to staff schools for the newly freed slave population; nontraditional black women educators such as Anna Julia Cooper, Maria Stewart, Ida Well-Barnet, and Lucy Laney. They all taught within a transformative framework, yet the concept was not separated from everyday living; rather, it was part of the reality of what it was to be black, trying to survive in an oppressive white-dominated society. Hence, our notion of transformation as a way of knowing, a way of being, and a way of surviving is grounded in a cultural legacy.

Grounded in an Oppositional Spirit

The sociopolitical dimensions shaping one's experiences are clearly evidenced in the dilemmas that blacks experience in America. As a group, people of African descent have historically occupied a position whereby we have constantly questioned our worldviews and our ways of knowing in relation to Eurocentric perspectives. In other words, we often live in opposition to the norm culture in that we inevitably negotiate between cultures. As a minority group who work and learn in majority cultures dominated by people of European ancestry, we constantly question our identity against markers set by European standards. For instance, we must recognize and grapple with the fact that a community with majority members of a dominant group will take on the values and mores of that dominant group and regard these as normal. At the same time, values and behaviors that do not mirror those of the majority are often viewed as deviant or wrong. Internally we believe in the values and mores acquired from our group socialization, but the dilemma results in the knowledge that if we adhere to these ways of knowing, we stand to be ridiculed and denigrated within the majority culture. The words of Sonia Nieto (2000), however, bring us back to the sociopolitics of power and privilege as they relate to our conceptualization and transformation of self in majority spaces: "The difference in perception is due more to the power of each of these groups than to any inherent goodness or rightness in the values themselves" (p. 140).

The negotiation between and across cultures is an integral part of the process of learning, critical reflection, and ultimately transformational learning and teaching for black women educators. According to Mezirow (2000), "learning is understood as the process of using prior interpretation to construe a new revised interpretation of the meaning of one's experience as a guide to future action" (p. 5). Although Mezirow says that intentional or incidental learning involves the use of language to articulate our experiences to ourselves or to others, we would emphasize the importance of providing a safe and supportive environment whereby students are free to articulate their experiences to others. It is through such communication and dialogue that we increase our awareness about the experience, learn to name it, and recognize the sociopolitical dimensions shaping that experience.

Here is an example of such a dilemma. Recently Mary was having a conversation with an international student from Taiwan. This was about their third conversation, and during their previous conversations the student shared her challenges as she made the transition to the culture of higher education in the United States. She said that prior to taking Mary's class, she was often mortified to enter the classroom because of her fear of talking in class, particularly since many of her teachers made oral participation a significant part of her grade. One professor told her in the presence of the class that she would fail her if she did not contribute to the classroom discussions. She shared many similar stories of humiliation, alienation, and marginalization in the classroom because she did not fit the profile of the "American student." What was most troublesome for Mary was when the student said, "I am so stupid; I don't know anything; somebody who cannot speak English is nobody. I don't feel good about myself here."

Because of the power we as American educators ascribe to the English language as a demonstration of competence, students of other languages internalize the English speakers as the ones with power to construct knowledge in what they perceive to be "an authentic voice." This is not surprising because as Minami and Ovando (2001) have found, "Most educational discourse and learning environments to date have tended primarily to reflect the discourse practices of mainstream society, with often unfortunate results for non-mainstream students, including many language minority students" (p. 427). Therefore, the ideological practices of the mainstream continue to adversely influence identity transformation among marginalized populations.

We must acknowledge that there are not ultimate truths or validity to the values that Eurocentric ideals imply; more important, we must manifest this knowledge in our own transformational learning and teaching within our classrooms. For African Americans and other minority groups who have their knowledge and worldviews discounted as irrelevant and whose experiences have remained marginal in the social science literature, such an approach to teaching and knowledge construction has promise for minimizing the dilemmas we face in white spaces. However, while transformational learning can be incidental, teaching for transformation must begin with a deliberate and conscious effort or strategy.

Most educators profess to value social justice, fairness, and equity and claim to demonstrate such values in their teaching. On close examination, we often find a disconnect between what teachers say they value and the values their practices demonstrate. As a result, we suggest reflections and transformation of self before we can begin to teach for transformation. In other words, in may be necessary for one to undergo some form of self-reflection and transformation in order to teach transformation. We must first examine and, when necessary, change our frames of reference to foster transformational learning (Mezirow, 2000). This process is critical because as Kegan (2000) notes, "Our frames of reference may be passionately clung to or casually held, so it clearly has an emotional or affective coloring. Our frames of reference may be an expression of our familial loyalties or tribal identification, so it clearly has a social and interpersonal coloring. Our frame of reference may have an implicit or explicit ethical dimension, so it clearly has a moral coloring" (p. 32). Kegan is suggesting that our frame of reference constitutes our worldview and ways of knowing. Therefore, unless we bring these into consciousness and understand how they inform our practice as adult educators, we cannot begin to teach for self and ideological transformation. As Clarke and Dirkx (2000) argue, "How we think and go about helping adults learn is shaped by how we understand the self" (p. 103). Knowledge of self therefore is a precursor to teaching transformation. We posit that it is this knowledge of self, constructed almost unconsciously and out of necessity in opposition to the larger dominant society, that makes transformational teaching and learning the air that we breathe and take for granted as the way to teach. Our past, our intellect, and our spirit have fused to produce a synergistic way of being that is coincidentally referred to in the literature as emancipatory and transformational.

A Balancing Act: Teaching and Transforming

Admittedly we are paid to teach and to transmit certain knowledge to our students. Embedding this knowledge in an environment that offers opportunities for transformation is our goal, but we understand that transformational learning cannot be guaranteed or forced on learners. We also understand that we do not own the high ground of truth or righteousness. What we are setting forth is that we try to provide a classroom setting where we engage with our students, our colearners, in critical reflection, critical thinking, reframing questions, deconstructing issues, and dialogue and discourse. Often in this setting we and others are renewed and transformed in the struggle.

The methods of teaching and learning that we use employ a political framework that attends to and encourages consciousness raising, activism, and a caring and safe environment. Implicit in this form of teaching, which is rooted in social justice, is a critique of Western rationality, androcentric theories, structured inequalities, and unequal societal power relations. In addition, the practices that flow from these strategies center on connected teaching (Belenky, Clinchy, Goldberger, and Tarule, 1986), in which the teacher and students jointly construct knowledge, engage in self-reflection, and practice self-revelation.

To achieve the classroom environment, it is important for us always to attend to classroom dynamics and classroom management. There are several primary methods that we employ in constructing this setting. For instance, it is important that no one voice, including the teacher's, dominates the discussion. We are not opting out of our role as the authority, but rather suggesting that as teachers, we attempt to guide and nurture the process of intellectual discourse. In addition, in our efforts to be inclusive, we recognize that students learn in different ways and also participate in different ways. Therefore, each class that we teach has varied instructional modes (printed materials, audio, WebCT components, video presentations, guest lecturers, collaborative and individual projects) and a range of other ways in which students can participate (suggesting curricular material, attending and reporting on relevant campus speakers, small work groups, games, and written and oral student presentations). We are successful as teachers if our students leave our course with more questions than answers and if we have helped them toward a lifelong self-directed learning journey.

In the environment of our classrooms, we attempt to encourage students to connect with or "trouble" the readings, always guiding them to examine their assumptions and the author's perspective and to query whose interests are being served. There are several ways to relate to the readings. One student-preferred way is to keep a journal or write reaction papers in which they analyze and critique the strengths and weaknesses of the author's arguments, but also use their personal experiences as a route for engagement. Regardless of the method, the act of interacting with readings gives students space to think critically and reflect on the ideas presented. Often they come to class with counterarguments and other sources to support or refute the readings. Ultimately what happens is that we all not only learn from the reading, but we learn beyond the assigned readings.

New Directions for Adult and Continuing Education • DOI: 10.1002/ace

Another strategy we employ in our classrooms is reframing questions and deconstructing issues. An essential aspect of producing this classroom setting is reframing questions (Brookfield, 1995) and asking students to examine issues on the micro, mezzo, and macro levels because the world extends far beyond the classroom walls to an ever shrinking global community in which we all must participate. As Brookfield (1995) recommends, reframing the question allows for the dissecting of the premise on which the question is based, showing that every question contains a position or perspective. If questions are only answered and not examined, then the opportunity to see behind the question is lost and simply answering the question is a form of reproduction.

Closely related to reframing the question is the postmodernist method of deconstructing or taking the issue apart. For example, in one class in a dissertation series, the class had occasion to examine the data of a student who was presenting her controversial study of women leaders in the Ku Klux Klan. One of the themes voiced by several of the Klan women as their reason for membership was the high incidence of blacks who commit crimes against whites. In deconstructing this issue, the class first offered statistics that most crimes are committed within racial lines and that only 17 percent of crimes are committed across racial lines. The points of deconstruction went on to include the imbalance of arrests and convictions along racial lines, the interlocking nature of poverty and crime, the disparity between sentences for white-collar crimes and blue-collar crimes, and the disparity of sentences between men and women who commit the same crimes. This means of dismantling an issue can expose the false or accurate components that make up the issue.

Perhaps the most often used and most successful building block of our transformational teaching is the use of dialogue, an informal conversational approach for verbal exchanges, or discourse, a more formal, linear, and directive methodology. It has been our experience that multiple voices, whether ordered as discourse or free flowing as dialogue, produce a symphony of ideas and lay groundwork that supports an environment where change is possible.

Conclusion

We are teachers, facilitators, and conduits for knowledge. While we are deliberate in our political positions of social justice, inclusion, and democratization, we are intentionally deliberate so as to be open and inclusive rather than oppressive. These ways of teaching, born from our marginality, exist in an effort to break the cycle that produced our outsider status. Perhaps in our teaching we are more vulnerable, but we practice from our soul, modeling the risks involved in being open to new ideas and allowing disparate voices to open up the path to growth and transformation. Such an approach keeps us steady on our lifelong journey as black women adult educators with a goal to "trouble" and, maybe, transform ideology and practice.

References

Belenky, M., Clinchy, B., Goldberger, N., and Tarule, J. M. *Women's Ways of Knowing.* New York: Basic Books, 1986.

Brookfield, S. D. *Becoming a Critically Reflective Teacher.* San Francisco: Jossey-Bass, 1995.

Clark, M. C., and Dirkx, J. "Moving Beyond a Unitary Self: A Reflective Dialogue." In A. L. Wilson and E. R. Hayes (eds.), *Handbook of Adult and Continuing Education.* San Francisco: Jossey-Bass, 2000.

Freire, P. *Pedagogy of the Oppressed.* New York: Seabury Press, 1970.

Johnson-Bailey, J., and Cervero, R. M. "The Invisible Politics of Race in Adult Education." In A. L. Wilson and E. R. Hayes (eds.), *Handbook of Adult and Continuing Education.* San Francisco: Jossey-Bass, 2000.

Kegan, R. "What Form Transforms? A Constructive Developmental Approach to Transformative Learning." In J. Mezirow and Associates (eds.), *Learning as Transformation: Critical Perspectives on a Theory in Progress.* San Francisco: Jossey-Bass, 2000.

Mezirow, J. *Education for Perspective Transformation: Women's Re-Entry Programs in Community Colleges.* New York: Teachers College Press, 1975.

Mezirow, J. "How Critical Reflection Triggers Transformation Learning." In J. Mezirow and Associates (eds.), *Fostering Critical Reflection in Adulthood.* San Francisco: Jossey Bass, 1990.

Mezirow, J. "Transformative Learning: Theory to Practice." In P. Cranton (ed.), *Transformative Learning in Action: Insights from Practice.* New Directions for Adult and Continuing Education, no. 74. San Francisco: Jossey-Bass, 1997.

Mezirow, J. "Learning to Think Like an Adult: Core Concepts of Transformation Learning." In J. Mezirow and Associates (eds.), *Learning as Transformation: Critical Perspectives on a Theory in Progress.* San Francisco: Jossey-Bass, 2000.

Minami, M., and Ovando, C. J. "Language Issues in Multicultural Contexts." In J. A. Banks and C. A. McGhee Banks (eds.), *Handbook of Research on Multicultural Education.* San Francisco: Jossey-Bass, 2001.

Mirza, H. S. "Black Women in Education: A Collective Movement for Social Change." In G. Ladson-Billings and D. Gillborn (eds.), *The Routledge Falmer Reader in Multicultural Education.* New York: Routledge Falmer, Taylor & Francis Group, 2004.

Nieto, S. *Affirming Diversity: The Sociopolitical Context of Multicultural Education.* New York: Longman Press, 2000.

JUANITA JOHNSON-BAILEY is professor of adult education in the Department of Lifelong Education, Administration, and Policy at the University of Georgia.

MARY V. ALFRED is associate professor of adult education and human resource development in the Department of Educational Leadership and Policy Studies at Florida International University.

New Directions for Adult and Continuing Education • DOI: 10.1002/ace

6

This chapter addresses ethical issues that can arise for an educator who ascribes to and practices from the theoretical perspective of transformative learning.

Ethical Demands of Transformative Learning

Dorothy Ettling

In a graduate class, we were enthusiastically discussing William Doll's (1993) views on adult education. The theory provoked excitement among the students and a sense of liberation as adult learners. So I suggested we experiment with his educational vision by redesigning our course functioning. It quickly became evident that this would entail a major reordering of some of the expectations, norms, and methodologies that some students were accustomed to and comfortable with. In a matter of minutes, we had the most heated and, I believe, most productive discussion of the semester. It was crystal clear that altering basic assumptions is fraught with fear and resistance even when the outcome may be a desired expansion of consciousness. I wanted to push this group to embark on the journey of change. I felt inclined to use my persuasive power, through gentle insistence, to encourage them to engage in the experiment. However, I did not. I was experiencing an ethical dilemma. On the one hand, these are mature, adult learners whom I believe have the right to organize their educational experiences. On the other hand, will they, without pressure, test the possibilities for new habits of mind? I face this situation frequently as an educator who intuitively sees the promise and the potential for transformative change in both people and events.

The short history of transformative learning theory has been sparked with both insight and critique regarding the seminal work of Jack Mezirow (1991). The development of transformative learning has grown from an initial emphasis on cognitive dissonance as the catalyst for critical reflection to include the role of other aspects of the human experience: emotionality, bod-

NEW DIRECTIONS FOR ADULT AND CONTINUING EDUCATION, no. 109, Spring 2006 © 2006 Wiley Periodicals, Inc.
Published online in Wiley InterScience (www.interscience.wiley.com) • DOI: 10.1002/ace.208

ily sensations, religious experience, subliminal and unconscious material, and group interaction in adult learning (Taylor, 1998, 2000; Cranton and Roy, 2003; Taylor and O'Sullivan, 2004; McGregor, 2004). Previous chapters in this volume have detailed the varied applications of transformative learning in adult education settings. This chapter proposes that the educator's engagement of transformative learning theory demands a conscious, ongoing examination of the appropriateness of methods that are used and the implications of outcomes that are fostered. This is, in fact, the ethical demand.

First, it seems important to disclose my personal milieu. As an adult educator who is committed to transformative learning theory-in-practice, I am simultaneously rooted in several contexts. One is the traditional world of academia. Another is an environment of practitioner scholars, searching to test and inform theory from the realities of the field. The third is a group of culturally diverse activists collaboratively striving for more peaceful, just, and empowered societies. It is from these contexts, mixed, jumbled, and sometimes contradictory, that I approach questions regarding the ethical implications of educating for transformation. Ethics, in my view, are the grounded set of beliefs that shape the appropriateness of my attitudes and behavior in any given context. That ground has been tilled throughout my life from a number of sources and is stabilized in all contexts by one central tenet: the dignity and the interrelatedness of all creation.

There may be no other period in U.S. history like ours, where educational reform is lauded and decried with such vehemence. Underneath the cries lies a spectrum of assumed aims for the educational endeavor with accompanying expectations of the educator. The educational goal for the students ranges from achieving personal success to accepting a global worldview, and the attendant task for the educator extends from preparing a person for the workforce to creating a planetary citizen. Wherever the educator falls within that spectrum, the educational experience is never value neutral. The position, perspective, and power of the teacher are always present in the classroom.

This added value is inherently linked not only to the educator's standpoint on the goal of education but also to her or his broader worldview. If one's educational vision is drawn from a predominantly modernist perspective that posits a closed system view of reality where cause and effect is the primary mode of relationship, a more linear and measured outlook on position, power, development, and change follows. If, however, one is influenced by the emerging postmodern framework of open systems that frames an understanding of change in both the physical and social worlds, another organic outlook is possible, focusing on interaction, disequilibrium, and equilibrium in the educational setting (Doll, 1993). It seems limiting to speak of transformative learning and the ethics involved in teaching from this theoretical perspective without adverting to, first, the educator's worldview and intellectual stance (for example, ethics as related to the purpose of education) and second, ethics as related to practice.

New Directions for Adult and Continuing Education • DOI: 10.1002/ace

Ethics as Related to Purpose

Is the primary purpose of education to impart information, construct knowledge, or initiate change? Sharan Merriam (2004) asserts that the "notion of development as change over time or with age is fundamental to adult learning theory and practice: furthermore, the direction of this change is almost always presented as positive and growth oriented" (p. 60). This implies a stage view of adult development and learner change. The basic orientation to adult learning as an individual endeavor long dominated the field of adult education. The contextual orientation, of more recent influence, stresses the learning context as an essential component of the learning process (Caffarella and Merriam, 2000). This perspective acknowledges that the learning process cannot be separated from the interaction that occurs in the learning situation with both instructor and fellow learners. Thus, structural issues of race, gender, class, and ethnicity are constituent elements of the learning situation and place ethical demands on the educational process and the educator. Can one ignore dominant behavior in the classroom? Does one openly address issues of accessibility or sharing of resources among students? Does the curriculum include underrepresented views or sources?

As early as 1985, Paulo Freire addressed the question of the ethics of transformative education. He asserted, "There is a strong, ideological dimension to this question of challenging and transforming the consciousness of students" (Shor and Freire, 1987, p. 174). Freire contended that the dialogical educator never has the right to impose his or her position but nonetheless should never stay silent on social questions. Freire's position was that a person changes her or his understanding and consciousness to the extent that she or he is illuminated in real historical conflicts. In fact, he claimed, "conflict is the midwife of consciousness" (p. 176).

Following a similar perspective, Derek Briton (1996) called for a "pedagogy of engagement" and challenged the adult educator to address the real problems associated with putting democratic and emancipatory ideals into practice in the classroom. Concretely, this view acknowledged that adult education is a sociohistorical and political practice, not a range of techniques and instructional methodologies devoid of human interest, and it demands an ethical base for one's research and practice. Edmund O'Sullivan's (1999) conceptualization of development in adult education is integral human development. He allies the deepest development of the self with the deep structure of the cosmos and makes a claim for an "ethical approach that can work for the species as a whole" (p. 223). According to O'Sullivan, what is needed is a series of guidelines that can be held in common by humans everywhere, regardless of race, culture, or societal status. Each of these viewpoints increasingly supports a consciousness on the part of the educator to recognize the dynamic nature of the learning situation and assume the responsibility inherent in a leadership role.

Transformative learning theory, according to Mezirow (2000), affirms the fundamental purpose of development in adult education and describes that development as "learning—movement through phases of meaning becoming clarified" (p. 69). Mezirow emphasizes that the role of adult education is to help "adults acquire the insight, ability and disposition to realize the capacity to engage in transformative learning" (p. 69). The elements in his description of the process have been summarized as an individual experience of a disorienting dilemma, critical reflection, and rational discourse (Taylor, 1998), thus stressing the primacy of the cognitive dimension of the individual learner. Numerous examples of practice in adult learning are contained in the previous chapters from the theoretical perspective of transformative learning, demonstrating how the theory has blossomed and expanded through application. More recently, practitioners and writers in the field are being influenced by explorations and findings in the biological and physical sciences.

With the advent of "new sciences" and the evolutionary theory of the universe, new theories of human development are budding and provoking a purpose for the adult learning process that includes both transformation and the growth of complexity (Doll, 1986). This view requires recognition of the web of interrelatedness that encompasses the universe and situates learning and transformation more as a set of emerging patterns than a process to be followed. It implies that a single unit can be studied but cannot be known fully unless it is studied as part of the larger whole of an organism. Thus, people are not understood unless their identity as part of the Earth system is also taken into account (Coelho, 2002). Brian Swimme (1984), speaking of our connection with the vast universe, writes, "The dynamics that fashioned the fireball and the galaxies also fashion your ideas and visions. . . . In your specific personal dreams and desire, the whole process is present in your personal self" (p. 135). It follows that the mind learns and creates from the human intelligence within a person but also from the patterns or fields that it shares with the larger world (Coelho, 2002).

Within this evolutionary frame, a transformative curriculum would be a process not of transmitting what is known but of exploring what is not known (Doll, 1993). Cavanaugh and McGuire (1994) comment, "Applying a chaos framework to lifelong learning is like taking much of what we already know and turning it on its head. Predictability is impossible in the long run. Stability is only temporary and is ultimately illusory. Confusion may even be a good sign in the right context" (p. 19).

Within these descriptions of adult learning lies the implication that both teacher and learner engage in a shared endeavor and that both are changed through this shared experience. Irene Karpiak (2000) claims that learners and teachers are "works in progress" (p. 41). This seems to place the teacher and the learner within the context of another worldview, namely, a participatory worldview, which may pose a different set of ethical questions for both. We now see new impetus and implications from the science of chaos theory. However, according to Karpiak, transformation as an orientation in adult education is still at the periphery of the field and receives far less attention than the more established orientations.

Ethics as Related to Practice

How does one decide how far to engage students in the practice of looking at underlying assumptions and beliefs? Transformative learning, as presented in this book, purports the perspective of adult education as a deeply engaged process. It presupposes a subjective awareness on the part of the student as well as a contextual relation between teacher and student and among students. My own work has reinforced the belief in the significance of context, and I argue for a holistic inclusion of the physical, cognitive, interactive, structural, and spiritual dimensions of the learning process (Ettling and Guillian, 2004). I describe transformative learning as characterized by evolving habits of mind as well as by new structures for engaging one's identity (Mezirow, 1991; Kasl and Elias, 2000) that recognize the interconnected web within the universe and accept the responsibility we share for one another and the earth within that web.

Although implications for practice may seem obvious from my descriptions, there is still a dearth of literature on how to operationalize the theory of transformative learning into the adult learning classroom or setting. Caffarella and Merriam (2000) reflect the questioning that filters through the writings of the reflective practitioners of transformative learning. Do educators have the right to ask people to examine and change their basic assumptions as part of our educational programs? Should one expect learners to seek this kind of learning experience? Is it justified to pose real-life dilemmas that force examination of one's life story and lived assumptions? And do adult educators have the expertise to lead participants through the transforming experience?

In a conversational article that focuses on teaching critical consciousness, Elizabeth Tisdell, Mary Stone Hanley, and Edward Taylor (2000) discussed the practical aspects of the ethical dilemmas of their transformative learning practice. Taylor notes, "There is little guidance and training in our field of how to deal with issues that often emerge from complex teacher-student relationships" (p. 143). Tisdell attempts to create a setting where students critically engage with the material and the process, but it is the students' decision to choose whether they do it. She approaches the dilemma by drawing up ethical ground rules for herself about how to deal with instructor power. For example, she never asks them to do what she is unwilling to do herself, she always gives students the option of observing and not participating in any experiential activity, and she clarifies that participants never have to share anything they consider personal if they do not want to.

In the same chapter, Taylor and Hanley comment on the exploration of provocative topics in the classroom. Taylor muses, "We can create conditions that promote a critical consciousness where participants' basic beliefs and values are called into question. That's where I begin to think about my ethical responsibilities of using the power as an educator to effect change" (p. 142). Hanley cautions the educator not to overstate the instructor power in the adult learning situation and recalls the larger context and dynamic nature of the learning process: "They [students] learn from each other, and then they take it out of the classroom and continue to make sense of what they learn. The important thing is that an educator gives students tools that they can use to live their lives" (p. 142). These authors contend, however, that there is minimal guidance in dealing with the issues that naturally arise in the context of transformative learning.

Elizabeth Lange (2001, 2004) has posed another perspective on the claim of ethics for the educator. She explored the potential of transformative learning for revitalizing citizen action, particularly action toward a sustainable society. She used action research with transformative learning to study how understanding develops in the midst of bringing about change. The participants studied their working and living, while the researcher studied the practice of critical transformative learning. What she discovered most significantly in this study was not disruption but restoration of the participants' foundational ethics to a conscious place in their daily lives. The basic ethics that people were taught and need to know were "submerged as horizons of significance over the adult life course. Restoring these learnings grounded the participants so they could withstand the disorienting aspects of transformation" (Lange, 2004, p. 135). In other words, it was not so much a new frame of reference that was created but a rediscovery of a submerged knowing. She names this "restorative learning" (p. 135) and states, "As the participants restored forgotten relationships and submerged ethics, they transformed their worldview, habits of mind and social relations" (p. 135). They in fact created a new or renewed ethic in their lives. Thus, she claims that engaging in transformative learning is an ethical act. The process itself "anticipates an enlargement of the sense of self" (2001, p. 88). By its very nature, then, ethical practice becomes an integral aspect of transformative learning.

Merriam (2004) has raised a different question that touches on the ethics of practice. She argues that "mature cognitive development is foundational to engaging in critical reflection and rational discourse necessary for transformational learning" (p. 65). She therefore questions the likelihood that most adult students possess either the maturity or cognitive development required to engage. One could then infer that to introduce the expectation of transformative learning primarily through critical reflection is an unrealistic and maybe even unethical, demand. She suggests there might be other models or contexts within which to situate transformative learning that reflect more a sense of interdependence and connectivity than the autonomous, independent thought usually associated with Mezirow's theory.

New Directions for Adult and Continuing Education • DOI: 10.1002/ace

Janet Moore (2005) recently questioned the context of higher education as a viable space for transformative learning to occur. Formal classroom structures are generally not conducive to reflection. Furthermore, she laments, radical departure from conventional modes of teaching is neither encouraged nor rewarded. Thus, is it ethical to expect it in this setting? Both of these queries are relevant and introduce the challenge of finding other ways of interacting with students and facilitating the transformative learning process.

All of this leads me to reflect on the insights gleaned from the "new sciences" touched on earlier. Within that context, Barbara Marx Hubbard (1998) has called us to a new evolutionary consciousness, one that embraces a social ethic in transformative education. When I dwell on the meaning of the learning experience from the perspective of a participatory universe, new questions confront me. What does transformation mean in this context of complexity? Who can name or interpret an educational experience as transformative? Finally, is the nature of transformation inevitably a mutually constructed, interactive process?

Conclusion

This chapter has presented a viewpoint that espouses the role of ethics in the practice of transformative learning. Adult education, with the intention of engaging a community of learners in a space for development and change, requires attention and integrity. Transformative learning, which implies a deep structural shift in one's consciousness and way of being in the world, presumes an authentic, value-based awareness. I close, then, not with answers to the ethical questions raised throughout the chapter but rather with the recommendation to each of us to develop a personal ethical creed. As educators, our first responsibility is to educate ourselves.

It seems important that we acquire an array of what might be termed ethical capacities. By this term, I am referring to competencies that can arise from the practice of intellectual, emotional, and spiritual rigor in our professional self-development, which then can offer us grounding and guidance in our everyday practice of transformative learning. Four that arise from my reflection are openness to cosmic awareness, an attitude of attunement, the art of conversation, and the practice of contemplation.

Openness to cosmic awareness is the capacity for ongoing critical reflection on one's own deeply held beliefs within an evolutionary consciousness. It calls us to recognize not only the multiple worldviews in a global community but also the possibility of rediscovering reality in the paradigm of a participatory universe. This capacity may challenge us to rethink the meanings of development and participation. It will most likely entail a stretch in our thinking and in our teaching so a new intellectual basis in transformative education can collaboratively emerge.

Attitude of attunement refers to the ability to listen carefully to what is voiced and unvoiced in the educational context. It includes, yet goes

New Directions for Adult and Continuing Education • DOI: 10.1002/ace

beyond, recognizing those who have been silenced and allows us to hear deeper levels of resonance and attend more fully to the complex sources of knowing within the human experience. It encourages us to find connection with others and align our awareness with action.

The art of conversation refers to the capacity to enter and remain in both the inner and the communal dialogue that is demanded as we explore new ways of understanding the capacity of the human experience for transformation and expansion of consciousness. It may well be that it is in the interaction that the transformative change occurs.

Contemplation, as a capacity, can be characterized as "a new way of seeing" (Coelho, 2002, p. 9), where "a vital relationship with reality's core is being discovered" (p. 78). The act of contemplating is looking in wonder at the possibility of the power for transformation in every aspect of our lives. Through contemplation, we realize that change cannot happen through reason alone.

Finally, I suggest we need new eyes and new hearts to truly address the ethical demands of education for transformation. The trajectory of this field in adult education is part of a much larger shift and leads us into uncharted territory. The journey cannot be guided solely by the ethics of rationality but will demand an affirmation of the spiritual, more mysterious dimensions of human experience. Companionship with one another, as we attempt to map this journey, will clearly be essential.

References

Briton, D. *The Modern Practice of Adult Education: A Post-Modern Critique.* Albany: SUNY Press, 1996.

Caffarella, R., and Merriam, S. B. "Linking the Individual Learner to the Context of Adult Learning," In A. Wilson and E. Hayes (eds.), *Handbook of Adult and Continuing Education.* San Francisco: Jossey-Bass, 2000.

Cavanaugh, J. C., and McGuire, L. C. "Chaos Theory as a Framework for Understanding Adult Lifespan Learning." In J. C. Sinnott (ed.), *Interdisciplinary Handbook of Adult Lifespan Learning.* Westport, Conn.: Greenwood Press, 1994.

Coelho, M. C. *Awakening Universe, Emerging Personhood.* Lima, Ohio: Wyndam Hall Press, 2002.

Cranton, P., and Roy, M. "When the Bottom Falls Out of the Bucket: Toward a Holistic Perspective on Transformative Learning." *Journal of Transformative Education,* 2003, 1(2), 86–98.

Doll, W. E. "Prigogine: A New Sense of Order, a New Curriculum." *Theory into Practice,* 1986, 25(1), 10–16.

Doll, W. E. *A Post-Modern Perspective on the Curriculum.* New York: Teachers College Press, 1993.

Ettling, D., and Guillian, L. "Midwifing the Process of Transformative Change." In M. Taylor and E. O'Sullivan (eds.), *Learning Toward Ecological Consciousness: Selected Transformative Practice.* New York: Palgrave-Macmillan, 2004.

Hubbard, B. M. *Conscious Evolution: Awakening the Power of Social Potential.* Novato, Calif.: New World Library, 1998.

Karpiak, I. "Evolutionary Theory and the New Sciences: Rekindling Our Imagination for Transformation." *Studies in Continuing Education,* 2000, 22(1), 29–43.

Kasl, E., and Elias, D. "Creating New Habits of Mind in Small Groups." In J. Mezirow and Associates (eds.), *Learning as Transformation*. San Francisco: Jossey-Bass, 2000.

Lange, E. A. "Living Transformation: Beyond Midlife Crisis to Restoring Ethical Space." Unpublished doctoral dissertation, University of Alberta, 2001.

Lange, E. A. "Transformation and Restorative Learning, A Vital Dialectic for Sustainable Societies." *Adult Education Quarterly*, 2004, *54*(2), 121–139.

McGregor, C. "Care(Full) Deliberation: A Pedagogy for Citizenship." *Journal of Transformative Learning*, 2004, 2(2) 90–106.

Merriam, S. B. "The Role of Cognitive Development in Transformational Learning Theory." *Adult Education Quarterly*, 2004, *55*(1), 60–68.

Mezirow, J. *Transformative Dimensions of Adult Learning*. San Francisco: Jossey-Bass, 1991.

Mezirow, J. "Learning to Think Like an Adult: Core Concepts of Transformation Theory." In J. Mezirow and Associates (eds.), *Learning as Transformation*. San Francisco: Jossey-Bass, 2000.

Moore, J. "Is Higher Education Ready for Transformative Learning?" *Journal of Transformative Learning*, 2005, 3(1) 76–91.

O'Sullivan, E. *Transformative Learning: Educational Vision for the Twenty-First Century*. London: Zed Books, 1999.

Shor, I., and Freire, P. *A Pedagogy for Liberation: Dialogues on Transforming Education*. South Hadley, Mass.: Bergin and Garvey, 1987.

Swimme, B. *The Universe Is a Green Dragon*. Santa Fe, N.Mex.: Bear, 1984.

Taylor, E. W. *The Theory and Practice of Transformative Learning: A Critical Review*. Columbus Ohio: ERIC Clearinghouse on Adult, Career and Vocational Education, 1998.

Taylor, E. W. "Analyzing Research on Transformative Learning Theory." In J. Mezirow and Associates (eds.), *Learning as Transformation*. San Francisco: Jossey-Bass, 2000.

Taylor, M., and O'Sullivan, E. *Learning Toward an Ecological Consciousness: Selected Transformative Practices*. New York: Palgrave-Macmillan, 2004.

Tisdell, E. J., Hanley, M. S., and Taylor, E. "Different Perspectives on Teaching for Critical Consciousness." In A. Wilson and E. Hayes (eds.), *Handbook on Adult and Continuing Education*. San Francisco: Jossey-Bass, 2000.

DOROTHY ETTLING *is professor at the University of the Incarnate Word, San Antonio, Texas, and director of Women's Global Connection.*

This chapter examines how the study of popular romantic fiction was used to transform students' understandings of the ways in which gendered identities are constructed and their perception of the way textual meanings are determined.

Using Fiction for Transformation

Christine Jarvis

> I think I see things differently, there are lots of things I see differently, now, with doing critical analysis.
>
> Louise, student

This chapter discusses learning that can be stimulated by engagement with fiction in the context of a structured educational experience. It is based on research that analyzed the experiences of women returners studying romantic fiction, both popular and literary. The research was stimulated by my observations of changes in understanding and attitude in previous groups, changes that seemed to go beyond increased knowledge and understanding of the texts themselves.

There is a diversity of applications and interpretations of transformative learning offered by practitioners and researchers (Taylor, 2000; Wiessner, 2004), but I am particularly interested in two aspects of transformation. First, I am concerned with transformations that enable learners to develop a critical awareness of social structures and powerful discourses and their impact on the construction of individual subjectivities. In terms of the framework originally developed by Mezirow (1981), these could primarily be termed sociocultural perspective transformations. Within that broad framework, they can be understood in terms of the analysis offered by

Accounts of the research have appeared in *Studies in the Education of Adults*, 1999, *31*(2), 109–123; and in *International Journal of Lifelong Education*, 2000, *19*(6), 535–547. They are reproduced here by permission of the editors.

Brookfield (2000) of transformative learning as ideology critique; he argues that "examining power relationships and hegemonic assumptions must be integral to the definition of critical reflection, thus turning it into a political idea" (p. 125). The second type of transformation consists of changes in what we believe about knowledge: how it is made and who can make it. These changes can be classified as epistemic perspective transformations. One of these types of perspective transformation is often dependent on or triggered by the other because beliefs about knowledge and truth and an understanding of political interest are intimately related.

I undertook the teaching on which I based the research in a college located in the United Kingdom with two consecutive groups of women, who were taking courses that provided preparation for higher education for adults without standard entry qualifications. Each teaching-research period lasted for one academic year and was recorded in my own participant observation notes, through in-course and end-of-course interviews, and in participants' own reflective journals.

The work we did in the classroom shared many of the features that underpin much transformative education, in that it challenged students' assumptions about the world and created experiences that confronted them with the uncertainty of knowledge. Greene (1990) argues that if the study of literature is to be emancipatory, there has to be some "ongoing intentional activity" (p. 265), by which I assume she means activity specifically designed to exploit the emancipatory power of textual study. Thus, while there is nothing unique about the way I teach literature, it is also possible to teach it much more didactically, so I have outlined here some aspects of the approach I took that seemed central to the production of the transformations the students reported.

As with any other such teaching, it was important to establish an environment in which students felt safe to air their opinions. I tried to do this by overtly stating that this was not a class in which we were searching for right answers, and we would be organizing primarily through small group discussions in which people would not feel too exposed.

I included time to develop the technical skills (often called close reading, or critical analysis) needed to understand the way literature is structured. This introduced students to the connotative properties of language and to features such as metaphor that challenge their beliefs about the singularity of meaning. This traditional approach to teaching literature proved a powerful tool that changed the way students "read" their worlds more generally.

We spent time on activities specifically designed to raise awareness of intertextuality, such as word association exercises, based on small sections of the set texts. Students explored ways they themselves gave meaning to a text by filtering it through other texts they had read and through the texts of their own lives and experiences, something Greene (1990) recognizes as essential to developing the transformatory power of literary study. In this way, they became conscious of the constructive role of the reader.

New Directions for Adult and Continuing Education • DOI: 10.1002/ace

They read varied critical readings, and I devised questions on these for their group discussion sessions to focus attention on contradictions between critics. This meant they had to confront the fact that authorities differed but also ensured that at least some of the readings challenged their own beliefs about, for example, women's roles, power in relationships, and the nature of pornography.

They were provided with questions relating to their set texts that expected them to look at sections in detail and discuss their treatment of questions such as power, identity, race, and social class. These questions helped them realize that meaning is not absolute but is made in a social context, determined by personal and political agendas. I framed these questions, and those about the critics, in terms that made it clear that it was appropriate to relate their interpretations and responses to personal experience; as a result, they explored the conflicts between their own perspectives on issues such as marriage, immigration, or feminism, and the perspectives in the texts they encountered.

I also built in creative writing sessions that gave students space to imagine alternatives to the kinds of discourses about women's lives and relationships that are most commonly found in popular literature. Texts included Mills and Boon romance novels (each student working with a different text and then making comparisons), *Jane Eyre* by Charlotte Brontë, *The Magic Toyshop* by Angela Carter, *Romance* by Joan Riley, and a selection of poetry. The object was always to have a critical dialogue—a dialogue with the text itself, between students, with imagined possibilities, and with teachers and critics.

Changes: The World and Their Place in It

The groups included women from different ethnic and social backgrounds; ages ranged from early twenties to mid-fifties, clustering in the early thirties. They came from a range of family and personal circumstances. They shared a belief that they had not fulfilled their educational potential earlier in life; most also had a limited income. My assumption, based on previous work with women's literature classes, was that many of these students would have read popular romances and that romantic discourses would be familiar even to those who had not. I also believed that these discourses are so prevalent that it would be possible for women from diverse backgrounds to make connections between the texts and their own experiences.

Over many years I had observed that women students often enjoyed these books but were embarrassed by their tastes. It was as though their emphasis on feelings, love, and relationships was shameful. This, for me, is connected to the way some feminist critics see the romance as a subversive form that resists a dominant social tendency to belittle those areas of life, such as marriage and the family, with which women are often associated in favor of the public sphere. Critics also note that the romance, with its focus on idealized heterosexual relationships, can be read as an expression of female dissatisfaction with the state of actual personal relationships with men. I hoped that the examination of romance through dialogue would confront us with our beliefs about and interpretations of our own experiences and demonstrate how the romance's dominant meanings have been influential but also resisted and subverted.

Dominant Discourses. The women were astonished by the widespread nature of the romance genre. They commented on aspects of romantic fiction commonly addressed by critics, such as its stereotypical representation of men and women and the heterosexist values it seems to embody. They noticed that these discourses insist that a monogamous heterosexual relationship is a prerequisite for being a "real woman."

Romance is so naturalized in our culture that we do not always recognize it as a powerful discourse; having studied it as a form, they saw it as a construct rather than as mere natural behavior. They noted how experiences they thought were unique to them fit patterns established by the romantic paradigm. Issues emerged such as relationships with older, domineering men—abusive relationships in which men's behaviors echoed those of romantic heroes. Laura, in her late twenties with two children, explained that the work we were studying was "a bit close to the grain": her ex-husband, "strong, capable," with "all the characteristics of a romantic hero," was actually "domineering and violent." Elaine, a married woman in her mid-fifties, believed that men themselves consciously attempted to act like heroes—until they had control of women, when they relapsed. Becky, a younger woman, felt she still accepted elements of the romantic paradigm because she preferred "powerful men." The process of reflection, however, meant she was probing the contradictions between this and her acknowledged desire to be "independent" and "rule the roost."

Marriage is the goal of all popular romantic heroines. Serena, a young divorcee, linked this to the expectations created in her own life when she talked about her drift into marriage, saying "it was taken out of my hands." Often the women spoke about their behaviors using words that suggested they recognized they were taking fictional roles. Louise, married for the second time after her first husband deserted her and her small child, described one romantic experience: "I would have said that somebody wrote that and we were acting in it." Abi, a young white woman, talked about being like a heroine by "*acting* very submissive." Sophie, struggling with an exploitative partner, noted that a few years ago, "I'd have tried to *act like a heroine,* just like little gestures they do."

Power in Heterosexual Relationships. As we discussed the texts, it became clear that many perceived power within relationships in purely individual terms. Through discussing these themes with others, they broadened that understanding to include the interaction of social and economic factors. I understood this to be an expansion of sociocultural meaning perspectives (Mezirow, 1981, 1990, 1991) from liberal, individualistic perceptions of personality and relationships to perspectives that acknowledge the significance of character and individuality, but recognize that these are socially constructed. For example, initially some of the women had not recognized the gendered social contexts in which the relationships were set. For example, Stella argued initially that women are powerful because they are desirable: "Porn actually shows the weakness of men who are exploited by women who choose to display their desirability for their own gain, thereby making men subordinate to women. . . . This all leads me to wonder if in fact women buy these books [romances] because they can interpret the endings to be the power they have over men to achieve their goals—marriage." This insightful reading of romantic fiction helps to explain the pleasures of the genre but neglects social and economic imbalances between hero and heroine that are integral to the thrill of subduing the hero. If he were not superior, rich, and powerful in the first place, gaining power over him would not be an achievement. Nor does Stella notice that the heroine's goal, marriage, is indicative of her limited options and may be a vehicle for her continued subordination.

These discussions about power often focused on arguments about whether heroines were strong or weak. It was here that we were able to recognize and respect the romance's capacity to value the emotions and its narrative insistence on making the hero place the heroine, the domestic and the personal, above his public success. Many women celebrated this reversal of the common order. At the same time, women began to see the contradictions in this position.

Women's arguments that heroines were strong often focused initially on individual strengths that would not be necessary had the heroines not been in weak positions socially and economically. For example, some argued that women held power because they chose whether to respond to men, ignoring the structural weakness of a position that makes them entirely responsive rather than active. Others said certain heroines were superior to other women because they won the hero, not noting the weakness of a social position that judges a woman's success by her ability to attract a man. Others admired heroines who were strong for resisting oppressive practices such as arranged marriages, but did not note the weakness of position that led to the need for resistance.

Toward the end of our time studying *Jane Eyre,* the students' responses to group discussion questions revealed their shifting perspectives. They started to discuss Jane's relationship with Rochester in terms of power as well as character and personality, as Becky noted: "The dependence and power balance has altered. . . . In the early part of the novel Jane is beholden to Rochester both financially and because she is his employee, therefore virtually having no power whatsoever in their relationship. The fact that Jane inherits a fortune puts her on a more equal footing."

Observations like this are commonplace in *Jane Eyre* criticism, but as the students discovered this for themselves, shifts in their understanding of structural factors affecting gender relationships took place that spilled over

New Directions for Adult and Continuing Education • DOI: 10.1002/ace

into many other aspects of their lives. For example, they began to question assumptions that were part of shared systems of belief within families. As is often the case when transformative learning takes place, friendships and wider family relationships were affected. They held less rigid attitudes toward social issues and were more inclined to consider situations on their individual merits. This meant they could not always share the comforting indignation of friends and family toward outsiders.

Changes: The Development of a Constructivist Approach to Knowledge

Hobson and Welbourne (1998) document a wide range of empirical work demonstrating that learners' epistemology develops with age and education, moving from a simplistic view of knowledge and right and wrong to one that understands it to be constructed. Explorations of such developments and their conditions have been important in the literature on transformative learning (Belenky and Stanton, 2000; Kitchener and King, 1994).

The study of literature can promote this development because it generally requires students to make meaning rather than receive it. Students began to read texts as a series of signs with shifting but often preferred or dominant meanings. This often led to an awareness that texts may be read as indicative of privileged values and beliefs. Encounters with criticism offering psychoanalytical readings of texts added to this understanding that knowledge can be constructed in the light of frames of reference that were not familiar to the author, such as psychoanalysis. Engaging with texts forced students to face the complexity of the connotative properties of language and the role of the reader in making meaning, so they could not sustain the belief that a text had a single right meaning or even a series of right meanings. This helped to foster transformative learning through critical reflection on the way meaning is made, particularly through challenges to the assumption that an author determines meaning.

Interpretation: Who Determines the Meanings?

The students mostly began by assuming that meaning belongs to the author of any form of communication. They saw studying literature as the process of finding out what the author really meant and went through stages that I think are familiar to many literature teachers. They initially believed that the meaning of texts is determined by the author's intentions, but that this was difficult to ascertain because of the difficult language writers use. Thus, the teacher's job, they believed, was to translate this language for the students. They then became concerned with hidden meanings that they felt had been planted in the text by the author and believed that teachers could reveal these hidden meanings. For example, after considering possible interpretations of one section of *The Magic Toyshop* and noting the many exam-

New Directions for Adult and Continuing Education • DOI: 10.1002/ace

ples of intertextuality that shaped our responses, Jill commented: "When I read a book I never spend so long on each page of the book so it makes me wonder why the author spends so much time putting so many hidden depths in."

Eventually most came to believe that meanings were not hidden but created, at least to some extent, by the reader, and were therefore different for each person. As their awareness of the impact of intertextuality grew, they made comments such as: "I never thought of reading as an active interaction between the book and myself. . . . In effect then, a book is not just one story but as many different stories as the number of its readers" (Stella). Aspects of the stages identified by Belenky, Clinchy, Goldberger, and Tarule (1986) could often be recognized as students moved, often erratically, from being "Received Knowers" (p. 37). They knew there were people called "critics" whom they thought had the right to decide meanings. They realized that some people, like examiners, had more power than others to legitimate students' readings, and this affected their ability to place their faith in decisions reached as a result of their own emerging "procedural knowing" (p. 129). One student explained during our interview, "Well, I have more confidence in myself now, interpreting it my way, even if no one else sees it that way. I have my reasons and it's like that, you know," suggesting that she was developing an epistemology based on procedural knowing, the valuing of reasoned arguments and evidence. Later in the same interview, however, she fell back into a more relativistic approach, expressing concern that her interpretation lacked value because she did not know if it was compatible with the approach taken by published critics.

The consideration of metaphor reinforced students' growing appreciation that words may have contradictory meanings and that they might need to accept these meanings simultaneously in order to come to a sufficient appreciation of the complexity and richness of a text. They discussed the contradictory and connotative properties of fire in *Jane Eyre*—for example, its capacity to suggest warmth and comfort, desire and sensuality, danger and destruction, and cleansing and purification. They often began by trying to "translate" metaphors by giving them an exact correspondence. In this case, they began by simplistically equating fire with love, then gradually noted all its other connotations. By the time they were considering the associative properties of fire in *The Magic Toyshop,* journal entries show that they read fire as destructive but also cleansing, dangerous but also just punishment. Their growing awareness of the complex referential properties of metaphor contributed to their enhanced appreciation of the complexities of determining meaning.

Some of the critical readings we studied implied that the unconscious is at work in literature. They sometimes contained implications about female fantasy that participants found uncomfortable. They also challenged the belief that meaning is made exclusively at a conscious level. Thus, they tended to unsettle assumptions about both the world (about female sexuality, pornography, childhood innocence) and knowledge. For example, readings of the popular romance that suggested it was a form of pornography were met by objections that romance writers did not intend to write pornography nor did readers want to read it. Many students believed pornography was dirty and disgusting and its users inadequate people. Thus, the emotional cost of accepting a critical reading that implied that they, or people they cared about, read pornography was high, and students found this both exciting and threatening.

Conclusion

Fiction can be used to encourage the development of particular kinds of transformation. Reading or watching fictions may do this, without the addition of an educational program. However, a structured program can focus on activities that encourage readers to take advantage of the transformative potential of fiction.

Fiction can offer the kinds of "disorienting dilemmas" that Mezirow and others have identified as triggers that start the transformative process. Thus, transformation is not dependent on the timing of a particular life event but can be stimulated by an imaginative event. This is more likely to occur if the fiction itself, and the themes explored within it, resonate for the students and can be related to important issues in their own lives. In this case, analysis of texts revealed contradictions at the heart of the romantic paradigm, subthemes within that paradigm, and their implications for gendered behavior.

Starting with fiction can be less threatening than a direct discussion of a theme. The research also indicated that students get the best out of a fictional encounter when they approach it through extended dialogue with others, as this increases the opportunity for contradictions and anomalies to emerge and be scrutinized. Activities, which in this case included the production of extensive individual reflective writings as well as group activities, need to provide opportunity for a critically reflective process that explicitly requires the making of connections between personal and imaginative experiences.

Transformative learning involves thinking beyond the taken-for-granted and considering how things might be different (Brookfield, 2000; Mezirow, 1990). Some fiction offers scope for imagining alternatives—different resolutions to familiar problems, alternative lifestyles, and moral choices. *The Magic Toyshop*, for example, led to some difficult debates that challenged taboos about incest. The student may not accept those perspectives, but the process of trying different viewpoints is part of the formulation of a new perspective. I found it useful to incorporate an element of creative writing, as this enabled students to struggle with the process of thinking beyond the narrative frameworks and dominant discourses that shape much popular fiction.

Textual study, by its very nature, challenges certain commonly held beliefs about knowledge and the making of meaning. These challenges can be enhanced if the teacher makes discussion of these explicit. Thus, the development of practical, critical, close reading is not merely a technical process but draws attention to the connotative and referential properties of language, to the role of the reader and of culture in making meaning (for example, what McCormick, 1994, calls the text's literary, cultural, and personal repertoires), to rhetoric and persuasion, and to the political nature of discourse.

References

Belenky, M., Clinchy, B., Goldberger, N., and Tarule, J. *Women's Ways of Knowing.* New York: Basic Books, 1986.

Belenky, M., and Stanton, A. "Inequality, Development, and Connected Knowing." In J. Mezirow and Associates (eds.), *Learning as Transformation.* San Francisco: Jossey-Bass, 2000.

Brookfield, S. "Transformative Learning as Ideology Critique." In J. Mezirow and Associates (eds.), *Learning as Transformation.* San Francisco: Jossey-Bass, 2000.

Greene, M. "Realizing Literature's Emancipatory Potential." In J. Mezirow and Associates (eds.), *Fostering Critical Reflection in Adulthood.* San Francisco: Jossey-Bass, 1990.

Hobson, P., and Welbourne, L. "Adult Development and Transformative Learning." *International Journal of Lifelong Education,* 1998, 17(2), 72–86.

Kitchener, P., and King, K. *Developing Reflective Judgment.* San Francisco: Jossey-Bass, 1994.

McCormick, K. *The Culture of Reading and the Teaching of English.* Manchester: Manchester University Press, 1994.

Mezirow, J. "A Critical Theory of Adult Learning and Education." *Adult Education Quarterly,* 1981, 32(1), 32–34.

Mezirow, J. "How Critical Reflection Triggers Learning." In J. Mezirow and Associates (eds.), *Fostering Critical Reflection in Adulthood.* San Francisco: Jossey-Bass, 1990.

Mezirow, J. *Transformative Dimensions of Adult Learning.* San Francisco: Jossey-Bass, 1991.

Taylor, E. "Analyzing Research on Transformation Theories." In J. Mezirow and Associates (eds.), *Learning as Transformation.* San Francisco: Jossey-Bass, 2000.

Wiessner, C. "Where Have We Been? Where Are We Going? A Critical Reflection on a Collaborative Enquiry." In C. Hunt (ed.), *Whose Story Now? (Re)generating Research in Adult Learning and Teaching: Proceedings of the Thirty-Fourth Annual SCUTREA Conference, University of Sheffield, UK.* Exeter, UK: SCUTREA and University of Exeter, 2004.

CHRISTINE JARVIS is head of community and international education at the University of Huddersfield, United Kingdom.

8

This chapter describes an innovative writing program at Simon Fraser University that has implications for fostering transformative learning.

Do the Write Thing

Adrienne L. Burk

"Amazing. I just realized what it's like to be a student of mine. It's nearly impossible." This comment came from a university professor recognized for his excellent teaching and award-winning writing during a process focusing on the linkages of writing, critical thinking, and pedagogy for an initiative at Canada's Simon Fraser University. As his remark shows, this process affected his awareness beyond simply rethinking course content or teaching behaviors. My contention is that this shift in awareness can be usefully understood in terms of transformative learning theory. To set both a material and a theoretical context for this chapter, I begin with a brief descriptive orientation to the university initiative and then position an analysis of it within a broader discussion of themes characterizing transformative learning (Taylor, 1998). I highlight three key findings that I argue contribute to an enhanced understanding of transformative learning, then consider some difficulties and reflections, and provide some concluding remarks.

Setting the Context: Simon Fraser University's WQB Initiative

Universities are places charged with the social responsibility for creating thoughtful, engaged, and communicatively competent citizens. To improve its commitments to these goals, one of Canada's most innovative comprehensive public universities developed and in May 2004 ratified a unique pedagogical initiative to raise undergraduate competencies in writing, quantitative reasoning, and breadth (WQB) (www.sfu.ca/ugcr). It is ambitious, envisioned as a project that will distinguish the learning and teaching cul-

NEW DIRECTIONS FOR ADULT AND CONTINUING EDUCATION, no. 109, Spring 2006 © 2006 Wiley Periodicals, Inc.
Published online in Wiley InterScience (www.interscience.wiley.com) • DOI: 10.1002/ace.210

ture at Simon Fraser University for the next generation. It is to span all three campuses in British Columbia's lower mainland and involve some 17,000 undergraduates, 5,000 graduates, and nearly 750 faculty (and their expected growth) through various activities and specifically through provision of courses reworked to address criteria in each of the WQB competencies. Of the three areas, by far the most challenging is supporting change in the area of writing, for evidence of critical thinking in writing goes far beyond what shows at a glance (matters of punctuation, syntax, and grammar). Instead, what counts in WQB courses is understanding how to use writing to show relationships of ideas, significance, and communicative effects. At Simon Fraser, we use a dual approach to support this. First, we help create and design multiple opportunities for students to use writing as a way of learning through various low-stakes assignments and activities (Elbow, 1997). Second, we use writing as a means of instruction; that is, we use both published texts and students' writing-in-process to highlight how, for various audiences and purposes, writing features different modes of reasoning, styles of address, effective uses of technical language, and presentation of evidence. This means that students in paleontology, for example, learn how to analyze data as a paleontologist, but also learn how to communicate that analysis differently for scientific peers, popular science magazines, and newspaper accounts.

The WQB initiative obviously involves many structural and pedagogical interventions. But how does it relate to transformative learning? Again, what appears to be at issue are the sociocommunicative effects of working with writing simultaneously as method and object of study. Consider how writing and critical thinking function in academic settings. Though taken together, they are a central activity of academic work (from all levels of faculty to all levels of students); approaches to learning how to write and think critically are often either ignored or border on the shameful ("don't ask, don't tell"). Instead, there is a tacit assumption in higher education that a peripheral spatial association "near" successful writers and writing provides sufficient mentorship. In particular, there are three deeply held institutional assumptions: that writing displaying critical thinking is structurally transparent, that assistance in decoding our own disciplinary discourse rules is pedagogically suspect ("I just figured it out when I was in school—why can't they?"), and that, in any event, a professor's job "is about content, not being a bloody English teacher." These assumptions prevail, despite the extent to which writing and publication are heavily employed in knowledge making and in furthering academic careers, and despite the fact that in an increasingly information-saturated and multicultural world, decoding texts is more complex than even a decade ago.

Challenging these assumptions involves working at both institutional and more intimate scales. To do this, a small academic unit, the Centre for Writing-Intensive Learning (CWIL), was founded in September 2002; I joined in 2003. To date, the three CWIL faculty have worked with some 120

New Directions for Adult and Continuing Education • DOI: 10.1002/ace

faculty and 400 graduate students in workshops, symposia, consultations, trainings, and collaborative writing projects. As well, we have worked with just over sixty courses (and several thousand undergraduates) in both upper and lower division across applied sciences, arts, education, and science faculties. To work with a course varies from low to high involvement, but at minimum features discourse analysis of some key texts (as to the way writing and texts function in the course, the discipline, and associated professional environments), consultation on the reworking of some assignments in a syllabus to incorporate iterative draft and feedback cycles, and postcourse faculty and teaching assistant (TA) interviews. High-level involvement involves direct interaction of CWIL faculty with designing an entirely reworked syllabus, teaching the TAs, and doing some direct teaching in the course classroom.

Thus, working with this initiative offers multiple points of intervention, from the informal encounters in the hallways, to seminar and workshop environments, to intensive consultations during course redesigns. It is these settings that have provided multiple vantages to assess the profound changes happening not just to the courses but to the faculty themselves as they revisit and rethink their own scholarly identities and pedagogical strategies. In reviewing cumulative raw data sets of field notes and interview transcripts, I am finding that transformative learning theory can be analytically productive for exploring the effects of WQB courses on faculty. What I suggest in the balance of this chapter is that this initiative, through its explicit focus on texts, both challenges and enhances transformative learning theory, as well as suggests how writing can be used as a tool to foster transformative learning.

How Is This Transformative Learning?

The transformative learning I see operational within the WQB initiative shares characteristics with all three of the major theoretical themes as outlined by Taylor (1998). The predominant aspects are from Freire (1970), with important caveats. Though certainly Canadian university students and their professors cannot be seen as members of an oppressed class (and this initiative is not a call to explicit political action), nonetheless, this initiative is very much cast to spark active critical citizenship beyond the life of the university. Furthermore, its methods are deliberately selected to demystify the transparency and dominance of cultural capital as embodied in texts and communicative repertoires. This is no small thing. For example, getting students to be able to analyze not only the content but the structure of presentation of, say, a public service announcement or a federal environmental policy statement not simply for what it says but also for how it has been constructed for effect involves a focused analysis of power, representation, and strategy. Finally, a WQB approach is fundamentally opposed to the "banking" theory of learning, in its iterative cycles of analysis of texts, creation, feedback, reflection on process, and re-creation. But the initiative is not only from Freire.

With both Freire and Mezirow (Mezirow and Associates, 2000), the approach shares an emphasis on recursive cycles of action and reflection, and on the blending of imaginative and personal, discursive and representational, and material and empirical domains. As is evident, there are no cataclysmic precipitating events in this initiative; rather, recursive iterations that occur are best described by Mezirow's ideas of "a series of cumulative transformed meaning schemes" (Mezirow and Associates, 2000, p. 7). However, the learning here is arguably both instrumental and sociocommunicative; WQB approaches always involve making thinking and textual analysis public and explicit. In this way, cognitive conflicts are encountered in cultural rather than psychologically individualized domains. As well, the resolutions of such conflicts are sought in communicative, as well as private, environments.

But there is also evidence of the third thematic area of transformative learning. As in all other forms of faculty development (Dan Pratt, personal communication, Spring 2004), this initiative is taken up by those at the extremes of the faculty career path—those at the beginning and those near the end of their professional lives. In that sense, there is a marked reflectiveness by a number of faculty about the importance of considering their life's contributions in a holistic sense—not just as teacher of content but as model, as mentor, as performative intellectual. In this sense, this initiative also shares some aspects of Boyd's work (1989; Boyd and Myers, 1988) in terms of encapsulating a reworking of the self as educator.

Focusing on Learning Rather Than on Teaching

The quotation at the beginning of this chapter comes from one of the faculty WQB workshops during a sketching activity in which professors are literally asked to draw on a page how they organize what they expect students to learn in a given semester. Many professors draw a weekly lecture-reading progression, punctuated by formal, evaluated writing exercises, exams, or both. Some, especially in sciences and performing arts, instead work to key events, such as field trips, artistic productions, or group projects. Others work "backward." One archaeologist, for instance, introduces in the first week the substance of what will be tested in the final week of the course, but uses the semester as a cyclical revisiting and deepening of analysis and interpretation. What emerges out of discussions of these approaches (professors are asked to hold up their sketches) are invariably marked by expressions of astonishment, delight, laughter, and studied contemplation. This occurs not simply because of the material evidence of so many different "right" ways of approaching teaching, but also because of the "aha!" of realizing how one appears to another. Also, this highlights for many professors what a thicket of supposedly obvious (but unstated) preferences undergraduates have to negotiate in completing written work across disparate disciplines.

Holding up such mirrors to themselves in the multidisciplinary settings of the workshops and seminars shows that professors, while assuming they are just considering rearrangements of course content, are actually engaging with repositioning themselves in epistemic terms. That is, they come increasingly to ask, "How does one come to learn?" rather than, "What should I teach?" A scientist, for example, was looking in a WQB workshop at an example of poor instruction designed to integrate contents of a table and a text, and said, "I do that all the time. I've been doing it for years. No wonder the students produce what they produce." Other professors in postcourse interviews suggested a slower realization of this epistemic shift about what students were learning and how this affected the faculty's understanding of structuring the learning process. One, a history teacher, remarked on what she was looking to evoke in the students' learning in her course on eighteenth-century France. She mentioned that she teaches students not a list of events and dates but a way of thinking about how history is made. She was immensely pleased with comments on students' postcourse surveys: "By the end of the semester, many of my students . . . [reported] that they felt what they had learned over the semester . . . was 'when I read the news . . . and I hear about France I have an informed position or [can] do an analysis of the situation.'" Similarly, a geography professor, while marking drafts of final papers, found herself deeply challenged as to what constituted her own scholarly identity and what counted as "prestige" disciplinary knowledge: "[It] was a challenge and very refreshing for me as a professor. . . . If a paper was weak, I had to think hard about 'what are three things that are really going to make a difference here?' and if a paper was strong, I was genuinely intellectually provoked. And that made me sort of question my own tacit values about what's good in this discipline, and what's personal opinion, and what's signaled in the professional literature."

The research on fostering transformative learning has typically focused on the student rather than the official educator-teacher who experiences and engages with such ontological and epistemological shifts (for example, Saavedra, 1996). The overwhelming evidence in this initiative, however, is that professors are consistently surprised, even shocked, when they realize how difficult it is to articulate just what constitutes successful communication and synthesis or analysis. This seems to reposition them in terms of their own ideas of what expertise they can claim, as well as how they interpret their students' work.

Domains of Engagement: Artifacts, Speech, and the Social Environment

Much of the transformative learning literature discusses the climate or environment of the learning sphere as existing primarily in a verbal or affective domain rather than a material one. The use of texts as "sites" to anchor conversations, of course, alters this (see also Jarvis, Chapter Seven, this volume; Neuman, 1996). I find the materiality of working with texts, however, strengthens the analytical capability of transformative learning theory. In the WQB initiative, the page is used as four kinds of sites: a rehearsal space (private), a semishared rehearsal space (as in peer review, journal, or drafting stages), a public rehearsal space (as when writing is displayed and analyzed for its successes for an entire class), and a display space (for evaluated, formal writing projects). These sites situate "artifacts" of conversations, which, while unable to capture the lived experience of those conversations, nevertheless offer something besides memory or psychological explanations for exchanges. Moreover, especially on specific pieces of work undergoing iterative cycles of drafting, feedback, reflection and redrafting, they serve as evidence of incremental alterations in the neurological changes of meaning making (Elbow, 1997).

Explicitly using the material site of the page also opens new educational and communicative domains. To write is to take ideas out of one mind and make them available for contemplation not just for the writer but for others as well. One professor blends the verbal and written domains in an intriguing way. In order to provide his students a sense of the way writing reaches the inner ear of a reader, he assigns written projects and clear criteria for success, but then reads aloud varieties of successful papers, openings, and conclusions to introduce students to the concepts of risk, invention, and originality that constitute the delights of unforeseen creative options students can produce. He says this allows him to be surprised too and to show students that texts are inherently social, even though we tend to think of academic writing as produced in conditions of isolation. In this way, he also reveals to students evidence of his own shifting positionality as expert, and thus approaches the horizontal alignment Freire (1970) discusses between teachers and students.

Another professor was trying for a similar effect by showing students examples of voice in academic writing. For her course on mass communications, she engaged in exhaustive trawling for writing in her own discipline; searched for sources in poetry, literary, and other social sciences; and engaged in discussions with colleagues and writers that could serve as examples. Tellingly, she could not find anything succinct that encapsulated the blending she sought of academic rigor and jewel-like prose that "we recognize when we read." It is all too rare. When she finally found something that approached a description and shared it with colleagues, they vetoed it as "too daunting for students." Is it any wonder students have difficulty producing strong academic voices?

However, both these professors, as well as some six others, reported that though many students could not, in the thirteen-week semester of the WQB course, actually master producing superior written work, they nevertheless displayed stunning progress in "deepening substance" of "questions," "class discussions," "student-teacher meetings," "e-mail peer comments," and "analysis of others' writing." In other words, the explicit focus on the structures of thinking evident in the texts allowed students much greater insights into their own interpretive, communicative, and creative abilities, even if they could not yet produce brilliant written texts. This again underscores that cultivating critical thinking and developing its expression in writing is not accomplished through a recipe-driven set of skills but instead is best achieved through a grounded, contextualized process.

What is intriguing about these observations is that they occur around artifacts—the texts themselves. The site of the page, because it forces an externalization of communication, wrests discussion away from the merely affective and psychological domains, and forces a kind of reconciliation with the material—an inherently perspective-altering, sociocommunicative activity.

Shifting the Boundaries

Transformative learning theory conventionally emphasizes individualism and individual learning; it relies on individuals as the locus of expression and evidence of transformative learning (that is, transformative learning is a self-reported phenomenon). WQB approaches appear to challenge and modify this focus, not least because, using the materiality of actual texts, the learning domain becomes an explicitly collective one (that is, discussions about thinking that show in writing are overtly, deliberately public). WQB approaches use the theater of the classroom for modeling critical thinking, stages of comprehension, and stages of response within a constructivist model. This challenges both students' and professors' preconceptions of learning and pedagogy.

This has had interesting consequences. One professor, adept with WQB approaches, came to rely on knowing the incremental deepening of each student's capacities for critical thinking and taught accordingly in the collective space of the classroom. When the next course enrollment was so large that it necessitated TA support, she was extremely distressed. "I don't know where I am with the course. I don't know the students. I miss them. I find it hard to position the lectures and assignments now." Another, a biology professor, claimed a different discomfort: "It's a big shift for me. Scientists *profess*. I'm not at all used to knowing about students." However, later in the semester, this professor, constructing a close analysis of a biology abstract to show students how it could be created, commented, "It never occurred to me to do this, and no one ever showed me. Why not? This makes it so much clearer what the biology is."

Alternatively, when professors have had considerable experience in teaching, they offer a different analysis. A mathematics professor, asked at the conclusion of a first WQB iteration of this course if he would use a WQB approach again, replied, "Hands down. I'd never teach it any other way. It was the most satisfying undergraduate teaching I've done in thirty years."

New Directions for Adult and Continuing Education • DOI: 10.1002/ace

And an economics professor noted, "You know, after forty years of teaching this course, I'm insecure in the sense that I usually go over a key list of technical concepts, and I tended to lecture them and then say, okay. I could see people falling asleep on the derivation of J-shaped evaluation . . . but now I don't do that. I say, okay, here is the visual on this, and you will discuss it in tutorial, or I may introduce it as part of the writing or something like this where I'm shifting the content of the course, not eliminating but shifting the content of the course." In both cases, the awareness of how they are teaching and of how students are learning is shifting, and it is traceable in terms of the material props of the assigned and produced writing.

It is also worth noting in the area of shifting boundaries that there appears to be a kind of hierarchy of disclosure among faculty about their own transformative experiences in undertaking WQB courses. In public spaces, faculty tend to mention writing difficulties or intentions in aggregated terms of pedagogical approaches or general patterns: "The class is doing well"; "Three students are struggling"; "About a third of the class didn't follow the assignment"; or, when speaking directly in a classroom to students, "Writing is hard; that's why we are paying attention to it here." In more private spaces, such as interviews or consultations with CWIL faculty, faculty members, by contrast, frequently disclose issues of their own writing selves: "I have such a hard time starting myself"; "I'm not sure how to do this"; "Writing is such hard work, isn't it?" Such conversations provoke a more focused, and thus potentially more vulnerable, exchange between faculty and CWIL faculty. This again opens spaces for more personal reflections for faculty as they are asked, "So, how does this assignment [or text or lecture] tie into what you said you wanted students to understand and produce?" "How does this assignment link to the reading?" "Can you recall how *you* learned this?" These more private exchanges not infrequently lead to disclosures by professors of bewilderment, frustration, surprise, and reexamination of their own scholarly identities and boundaries of expertise.

A Note on Challenges

There are, of course, examples of WQB approaches that are less suggestive than those already mentioned. Some professors who have undertaken WQB courses refuse to engage at the levels shown here, preferring to download the whole process to TAs, or they persist in regarding the initiative as about grammar rather than developing critical thinking. There are professors who claim they have "too much content to bother" with what they see as too time intensive a process. And indeed, the time involved is an important issue, though it is more one of rearranged rather than increased time commitment (as the economics professor noted). In fact, it appears that the time involved is directly related to the preparation timing for reworking a course.

There are generally three points at which faculty have the opportunity to reflect most intensely on using WQB approaches. CWIL provides faculty and TA training every semester to preempt difficulties in undertaking a WQB course. If faculty participate in these workshops, they begin early on to rethink what it is they want students to learn. This stage involves looking for (or inventing) texts and templates that model the desired criteria, and working to redesign assignments and syllabi. For the most thoughtful preparation, this process can take up to a year; generally professors allow themselves part of a semester. And others choose simply to jump in. During the semester, the reflections often center on the shifts in dynamics between faculty and students as mentioned above (in the example of the history and the biology professors). These dynamics often relate to confusion or a sense of obligation about how to respond at both a content and a process level to students' written work (as in the geography professor's comment earlier). Also, if there are TAs, they often require similar guidance. It is usually during the second iteration of a WQB course (or following a "just-in-time" training on how to respond to drafts) where this time demand is tamed. A third stage of reflection comes at the end of the course and in the subsequent months. Here, faculty share a veteran's knowledge of what is involved in WQB courses in informal settings—first in individual postcourse interviews about their experiences and then in CWIL-sponsored end-of-semester lunches where those about to teach a WQB course get to meet and exchange tips with those just finishing one. There are also, of course, ad hoc encounters around the university and the sharing of templates and guides developed in one course with others. There may be another stage of reflection, yet to be discovered. A perspective shift is often a slow realization. It is quite possible, given that this initiative is so new, that practitioners do not even yet recognize fully their own changes, and so are not yet able to articulate them.

It should also be noted that even with the official university interest in this initiative, institutionality itself deeply affects professors' abilities to undertake a pedagogical shift. This initiative relates to disciplinary knowledge; it is therefore subject to the various organizational and disciplinary cultures that shape university practices. Such cultures vary dramatically across the university in their receptivity to the ideas of decoding expert knowledge and pedagogic innovation (Bernstein, 1971). They also vary in emphasis on teaching rather than research. Furthermore, the initiative has been undertaken in a time of tremendous instability in teaching staff. At this university, as at many others, limited-term faculty and sessional lecturers comprise nearly 50 percent of the teaching staff. Finally, the WQB initiative has been launched within an economic and political climate that demands taxpayer accountability and vocational competence of graduates. All of these impose demands and set horizons of expectations on who can reflect, and about what. These constraints are genuine and are perhaps better understood by more suprapersonal theories than transformative learning, such as frame factor theory, which explains how apparently individually chosen pedagogic innovations can instead be seen as manifestations of deeper structural processes (see, for example, Nesbit, 1998).

Conclusion

This chapter has introduced an interesting pedagogical experiment—Simon Fraser University's WQB initiative—and suggests how it is unfolding in ways that offer some extensions of transformative learning theory. The nature of this initiative is that it inherently focuses on a series of small, iterative changes in meaning schemas as represented most concretely in exchanges of texts. Transformative learning therefore is precipitated by incremental rather than dramatic events. What is a slightly surprising finding, however, is that these iterative changes, intended for students, appear to also reposition faculty, not only at a cerebral level but also affectively, socially, and imaginatively. Their identities as scholars, as educators, and as persons are all subject to intense reflection within a social understanding, as both their actions and their reflections in this initiative are on show.

The initiative is new and still emerging. Deeper analysis of the data collected anecdotally and in field notes, surveys, products, and institutional exchanges is ongoing and will yield new findings. What is already apparent, however, is that using the materiality of texts as both object and method of research opens new opportunities for transformative encounters. First, using formal texts as instantiations of accepted cultural practices that can be publicly analyzed for both content and structure allows for interactive discussions of what constitutes knowledge, representation, faculty expertise, and persuasive communication. Second, for faculty to articulate to themselves and to others what constitutes powerful, effective, correct, and nuanced writing in their areas of expertise forces an epistemic shift from "What can I teach?" to "How can this be learned?" And third, the sharing of draft texts in stages enlarges the sociocommunicative realm and allows expertise to be seen as a flexible and contextualized phenomenon. Together, these suggest that anchoring transformative learning to material as well as affective domains shows considerable promise for extensions to transformative learning theory.

References

Bernstein, B. "On the Classification and Framing of Educational Knowledge." In M. Young (ed.), *Knowledge and Control: New Directions for the Sociology of Education*. London: Crowell Collier & Macmillan, 1971.

Boyd, R. D. "Facilitating Personal Transformation in Small Groups, Part I." *Small Group Behavior*, 1989, *20*, 459–474.

Boyd, R. D., and Myers, J. G. "Transformative Education." *International Journal of Lifelong Education*, 1988, *7*(4) 261–284.

Elbow, P. "High Stakes and Low Stakes in Assigning and Responding to Writing." In M. D. Sorcinelli and P. Elbow (eds.), *Writing to Learn: Strategies for Assigning and*

Responding to Writing Across the Disciplines. New Directions for Teaching and Learning, no. 69. San Francisco: Jossey-Bass, 1997.

Freire, P. *Pedagogy of the Oppressed.* New York: Seabury Press, 1970.

Mezirow, J., and Associates (eds.). *The Transformative Power of Learning.* San Francisco: Jossey-Bass, 2000.

Nesbit, T. "Teaching in Adult Education: Opening the Black Box." *Adult Education Quarterly,* 1998, *48*(3), 157–170.

Neuman, T. P. "Critically Reflective Learning in a Leadership Development Context." Unpublished doctoral dissertation, University of Wisconsin, 1996.

Saavedra, E. "Teachers' Study Groups: Contexts for Transformative Learning and Action." *Theory into Practice,* 1996, *35,* 271–277.

Taylor, E. W. *Transformative Learning: A Critical Review.* Information Series no. 374. Columbus, Ohio: ERIC Clearinghouse on Adult, Career, and Vocational Education, 1998.

ADRIENNE L. BURK is acting director of the WQB Initiative at Simon Fraser University, Vancouver, British Columbia, Canada.

New Directions for Adult and Continuing Education • DOI: 10.1002/ace

In summarizing the shared themes of the authors of the previous chapters, this chapter explores the role of the transformative educator, the transformative classroom environment, the transformative text, and the student when teaching for change.

The Challenge of Teaching for Change

Edward W. Taylor

After looking back over the previous eight chapters, a number of thoughts come to mind when I think about fostering transformative learning in my classroom. Admittedly I do not feel any less challenged by the task after reflecting on the information in the text, but I do feel more reassured that the practice of transformative learning, teaching for change, is an admirable approach to teaching and offers tremendous potential for growth among my students and myself as an educator, if I am willing to take some risks. Furthermore, what is interesting about the experiences shared in this volume is that despite the variety of interpretations in the meaning and purpose of transformative learning, there are significant streams of commonality in how these authors described the role of the transformative educator, the classroom environment, and methods that foster personal and social change. By discussing these commonalities, I hope to reveal a richer picture of some of the significant challenges associated with the practice of fostering transformative learning and innovative methods in order to help others become better educators of adult learners. Four areas in particular emerge that warrant further discussion: the transformative educator, the transformative classroom environment, the transformative text, and the transformative student.

The Transformative Educator

Wearing the title or moniker of transformative educator should not be taken lightly or without considerable personal reflection. Although the rewards may be great for both the teacher and the learner, it demands a great deal work, skill, and courage. Johnson-Bailey and Alfred (Chapter Five) bring clarity to

the most significant challenge associated with the role of a transformative educator by going so far as to say that it "may be necessary for one to undergo some form of self-reflection and transformation in order to teach transformation." It means asking, Are we willing to transform ourselves in the process of helping our students transform? One could therefore take the position that without developing a deeper awareness of our own frames of reference and how they shape our practice, there is little likelihood that we can foster change in others. Davis-Manigaulte, Yorks, and Kasl remind us in Chapter Three of "the importance of being fully present in [your] relationships with learners and about being fully grounded in [your] own multiple ways of knowing."

Despite this need to transform, however, it seems possible that we can also be personally affected by our transformative practice, even though that may not be our intent. As Burk (Chapter Eight) described the shift in perspective among the faculty who were successful at implementing the WQB intensive writing program, it seemed that many entered the project unaware of the impact it would have on their view of teaching and learning. So the choice of being transformed may not always reside with the educator. Developing this awareness about our practice and ourselves is not easy, but fortunately we are provided some guidance in this text.

One way to make sense of becoming a transformative educator is to think of it as developing a more authentic teaching practice. Drawing on the work of a number of authors, we can see that an authentic practice seems to be multidimensional, where educators develop a greater awareness of the self (both personal and cultural), an appreciation of the spiritual, and a recognition of the ethical dimensions associated with fostering transformative learning. In Chapter One, Cranton provides the most definitive work on authenticity and teaching, offering thoughtful strategies to help educators develop a greater self-awareness, awareness of others, specifically students, and an appreciation of how context shapes that process. Her work is an excellent beginning point for the journey of exploring authenticity, but there are additional signposts that need to be addressed and reflected upon along the way.

In particular for those of us from a Eurocentric background, it means developing an appreciation of our own culture and the associated privileges and powers. Like Johnson-Bailey and Alfred's perspective on transformative learning, it means understanding my cultural journey in becoming an educator and how my cultural background shapes my frame of reference. It means asking such questions as, How does being white shape my approach to teaching, and my choice of curriculum? And which students do I most identify with in my classes? A means to greater cultural awareness in relationship to authenticity can be found in Chapter Four by Tolliver and Tisdell. By exploring and sharing the symbols, images, and ways of being that are most significant in your life, a spiritual dimension begins to emerge in your transformative practice, leading to greater authenticity, openness, and acceptance by others.

Finally, an area that is rarely discussed but that I believe is essential to an authentic practice is developing an appreciation for the ethical responsibilities

New Directions for Adult and Continuing Education • DOI: 10.1002/ace

associated with the practice of transformative learning. Ettling nicely brings the ethical dimension to the fore in Chapter Six by encouraging readers to reflect on the ethics related to both the purpose and practice of transformative education. More specifically, it is recognizing that "the educational experience is never value neutral. The position, perspective, and power of the teacher are always present in the classroom." Accepting this premise means developing an understanding of the political agenda that undergirds your practice and being aware of the related consequences for both the students and teacher in the engagement of transformative learning.

Transformative Classroom Environment

Along with working toward a more authentic practice, another factor emerged: the importance of providing a safe, inclusive, and open learning environment. Without a healthy learning environment, transformative learning is stifled and rarely achieved. Although this premise is not new in relationship to what is known about fostering transformative learning, much more detail about what makes a transformative environment is revealed in this text. For example, the classroom environment needs to broaden its agenda beyond the narrow confines of a traditional cognitive orientation to learning and lead to an exploration of multiple knowledge productions, inclusive of the affective and relational and the symbolic, spiritual, and imaginative domains of learning, as Tolliver and Tisdell explore in Chapter Four. A good example of a more inclusive environment is revealed through a description of presentational knowing by Davis-Manigaulte, Yorks, and Kasl: "Presentational ways of knowing include the engagement with music, all the plastic arts, dance, movement, and mime, as well as all forms of myth, fable, allegory, story, and drama."

Most significant, presentational knowing provides the transformative educator imaginative with ways to engage emotional issues often found within transformative learning experiences. Long the stepchild in exploration of the cognitive dimensions of teaching and learning, the affective domain within the classroom can reveal much about the psycho- and sociocultural dynamics of the individual and the group. Engaging emotions in the classroom provides "an opportunity for establishing a dialogue with those unconscious aspects of ourselves seeking expression through various images, feelings, and behaviors within the learning setting," as Dirkx notes in Chapter Two. Furthermore, Dirkx continues, by exploring unconscious emotional issues with students, the educator will often not only address the dynamics that contribute to a resistance in learning, but potentially initiate a process of individuation—"a deeper understanding, realization, and appreciation of who he or she is."

In addition to including expressive ways of knowing beyond the rational, two other essential factors of the transformative classroom environment emerge: ritual and reciprocity. Ritual is not just offering a sense of routine and repetitive behavior; it is also being "intentionally more inclusive of the spiritual and appreciative of various cultural expressions" (Tolliver and Tisdell).

New Directions for Adult and Continuing Education • DOI: 10.1002/ace

More specifically, it means creating mechanisms in the classroom that foster social significance not only for gathering and closing a classroom session, but rituals during the class that foster collective opportunities of making meaning.

In addition to ritual, an ideal transformative learning environment is built on reciprocity. Reciprocity is based on that golden rule that is what is good for the goose is good for the gander. As we honor and draw out the wealth of personal knowledge our students bring to the classroom experience, challenging them to reflect critically, we also must demonstrate what Johnson-Bailey and Alfred refer to as a willingness to "engage in personal critical reflection with the students and to evoke the interdependency that makes the process of transformational learning and teaching transparent and synergistic."

Transformative Text

Beyond the transformative educator and classroom environment, one of the most fascinating discussions that emerged from these chapters is the power of text in fostering transformative learning. The predominant manifestation of text in transformative learning for most of the authors is seen in the form of providing course readings that offer a basis for small group dialogue and class discussions. Burk, Jarvis, and Dirkx, in three separate chapters, reveal in much greater depth how text can help facilitate what Jarvis describes as the "way students 'read' their worlds" and contribute to transforming perspectives.

Through the WQB initiative that Burk describes, an emphasis on writing and reflection shifts the sphere of transformative learning from one primarily residing in the context of dialogue to the materiality of text. This shift to the material is argued to possibly strengthen the analytical capability often associated with transformative learning. The material sphere opens up new forms of communication, creating artifacts of ideas of the mind and making them available for others beyond the individual writer to analyze and contemplate. In essence, writes Burk, it "forces an externalization of communication, wrests discussion away from the merely affective and psychological domains, and forces a kind of reconciliation with the material—inherently perspective altering, sociocommunicative activity."

Similarly, Jarvis introduces us to another genre of text not generally engaged in the halls of adult education, that of romantic fiction, as a medium for women to develop an awareness of how social structures and related discourses influence their frames of reference. These narratives become a place, similar to most other course readings, to "anchor conversation." In this case, the use of romance novels was found to be less threatening than a direct discussion about the topic in class. In essence, the text becomes an encounter with a third person in a classroom dialogue, where the learners discuss their own perspective in relationship to the narrative. Furthermore, as Dirkx brings to the light, the text for some students offers a doorway to deeply held emotions with the potential to initiate a process of individuation, a transformative experience.

New Directions for Adult and Continuing Education • DOI: 10.1002/ace

Also, in Jarvis's approach, similar to Burk's iterations of writing, the text is seen as having not a single meaning but multiple meanings, like multiple perspectives, that foster greater critical reflection. Finally, this process also raises the questions about what and who determines meaning, thus encouraging greater epistemological sophistication among learners.

Transformative Student

Embedded in this affirmation of and ongoing work on fostering transformative learning, there are still significant areas of practice that need greater clarity and understanding. In particular, there needs to be discussion about the learner's role and his or her inherent responsibilities in the transformative classroom. Accepting that there is risk for all involved in the process, understanding the learner's responsibility when fostering transformative learning becomes that much more an imperative. It means exploring important questions with students—for example: What is the student's role when it comes to promoting learning in the classroom? What is the student's role in monitoring and ensuring a safe learning environment?

Along with the learner's responsibilities there is a need to develop a better understanding of learner resistance to transformative learning. In particular, there needs to be discussion about such questions as, How does resistance manifest in the transformative classroom? Why do some students openly engage in this process, while others refuse to participate? What can transformative educators do in their practice to lessen resistance among students? A number of developmental, cultural, and institutional factors, all of which need further investigation, could explain resistance among students.

Conclusion

The efforts of this volume's authors affirm to a great extent the power of transformative learning as a practice and its potential for fostering change in the classroom for both learners and educators. Thanks to these authors, we have a much deeper understanding of the role of the transformative educator, the meaning of an authentic practice, the essential aspects of a transformative classroom environment, and how text can be used as a tool for transformation. Also, there is a growing appreciation for the role of culture and how diversity through the realm of the spiritual can be a medium to foster change and understanding among learners. Furthermore, we are beginning the process of engaging a discussion on ethical questions associated with transformative learning and the related consequences it has for learners and educators.

EDWARD W. TAYLOR is associate professor at Penn State University Harrisburg, Middletown, Pennsylvania.

Back Issue/Subscription Order Form

Copy or detach and send to:

Jossey-Bass, A Wiley Imprint, 989 Market Street, San Francisco, CA 94103-1741

Call or fax toll-free: Phone 888-378-2537 6:30AM – 3PM PST; Fax 888-481-2665

Back Issues: Please send me the following issues at $29 each
(Important: please include series initials and issue number, such as ACE96.)

_____

_____

_____

$ _____   Total for single issues

$ _____   SHIPPING CHARGES: SURFACE   Domestic   Canadian
                                   First Item $5.00 $6.00
                                   Each Add'l Item $3.00 $1.50
                        For next-day and second-day delivery rates, call the number listed above.

Subscriptions: Please __start __renew my subscription to *New Directions for Adult and Continuing Education* for the year 2____ at the following rate:

U.S.	__Individual $80	__Institutional $180
Canada	__Individual $80	__Institutional $220
All Others	__Individual $104	__Institutional $254

**For more information about online subscriptions visit
www.interscience.wiley.com**

$ _____   Total single issues and subscriptions (Add appropriate sales tax for your state for single issue orders. No sales tax for U.S. subscriptions. Canadian residents, add GST for subscriptions and single issues.)

__Payment enclosed (U.S. check or money order only)
__VISA __MC __AmEx #_____ Exp. Date _____

Signature _____ Day Phone _____
__ Bill me (U.S. institutional orders only. Purchase order required.)

Purchase order # _____
                 Federal Tax ID13559302   **GST 89102 8052**

Name _____

Address _____

_____

Phone _____ E-mail _____

For more information about Jossey-Bass, visit our Web site at www.josseybass.com

**NEW DIRECTIONS FOR
ADULT AND CONTINUING EDUCATION
IS NOW AVAILABLE ONLINE AT WILEY INTERSCIENCE**

What is Wiley InterScience?

Wiley InterScience is the dynamic online content service from John Wiley & Sons delivering the full text of over 300 leading scientific, technical, medical, and professional journals, plus major reference works, the acclaimed *Current Protocols* laboratory manuals, and even the full text of select Wiley print books online.

What are some special features of Wiley InterScience?

Wiley InterScience Alerts is a service that delivers table of contents via e-mail for any journal available on Wiley InterScience as soon as a new issue is published online.
Early View is Wiley's exclusive service presenting individual articles online as soon as they are ready, even before the release of the compiled print issue. These articles are complete, peer-reviewed, and citable.
CrossRef is the innovative multi-publisher reference linking system enabling readers to move seamlessly from a reference in a journal article to the cited publication, typically located on a different server and published by a different publisher.

How can I access Wiley InterScience?

Visit http://www.interscience.wiley.com

Guest Users can browse Wiley InterScience for unrestricted access to journal Tables of Contents and Article Abstracts, or use the powerful search engine.
Registered Users are provided with a *Personal Home Page* to store and manage customized alerts, searches, and links to favorite journals and articles. Additionally, Registered Users can view free Online Sample Issues and preview selected material from major reference works.
Licensed Customers are entitled to access full-text journal articles in PDF, with select journals also offering full-text HTML.

How do I become an Authorized User?

Authorized Users are individuals authorized by a paying Customer to have access to the journals in Wiley InterScience. For example, a university that subscribes to Wiley journals is considered to be the Customer. Faculty, staff and students authorized by the university to have access to those journals in Wiley InterScience are Authorized Users. Users should contact their Library for information on which Wiley journals they have access to in Wiley InterScience.

ASK YOUR INSTITUTION ABOUT WILEY INTERSCIENCE TODAY!